I have known Barry Miller
teaching and wisdom he h
proven to be both inspiring

For as long as I've known Barry he has been passionate about his study of the biblical cycles, their connection to the economy, world events, and everyday life. I expect his book to be both thought provoking and impactful for making better decisions.

Profound truths...evident in the days of creation, woven into the fabric of history, shaping my perspective and decisions today regarding tomorrow.

God is the Creator. Order began with Him, as did love and relationship. God is always, always good. He has established principles, such as gravity, that impact us regardless of our awareness or acknowledgment. In the following pages, Barry Miller brings clarity to truths around God's order that are impacting our lives. From Genesis through tomorrow, God reveals Himself in a consistent manner. An invitation has been extended to gain a deeper understanding of how to live in accordance with God's seasons, cycles, and celebrations.

KNOW THE
TIME
CHANGE YOUR
WORLD

KNOW THE TIME CHANGE YOUR WORLD

BARRY L. MILLER

CREATION
HOUSE

KNOW THE TIME, CHANGE YOUR WORLD by Barry Miller
Published by Creation House
A Charisma Media Company
600 Rinehart Road
Lake Mary, Florida 32746
www.charismamedia.com

Unless otherwise noted, all Scripture quotations are from the New American Standard Bible. Copyright © 1960, 1962, 1963, 1968, 1971, 1972, 1973, 1975, 1977, 1995 by the Lockman Foundation. Used by permission. (www.Lockman.org)

Scripture quotations marked NKJV are from the New King James Version of the Bible. Copyright © 1979, 1980, 1982 by Thomas Nelson, Inc., publishers. Used by permission.

Scripture quotations marked SCHOCKEN are from Everett Fox, trans., *The Schocken Bible, Volume 1: The Five Books of Moses: Genesis, Exodus, Leviticus, Numbers, Deuteronomy* (New York: Schocken Books, 1995).

Design Director: Justin Evans
Cover design by Nathan Morgan

Visit the author's website: 7and5orhymes.com.

Library of Congress Cataloging-in-Publication Data:
2015934810
International Standard Book Number (hardback):
978-1-62998-439-1
International Standard Book Number (paperback):
978-1-62998-437-7
E-book International Standard Book Number:
978-1-62998-438-4

While the author has made every effort to provide accurate telephone numbers and Internet addresses at the time of publication, neither the publisher nor the author assumes any responsibility for errors or for changes that occur after publication.

First edition

15 16 17 18 19 — 9 8 7 6 5 4 3 2 1
Printed in Canada

*For Herschel and Georgia,
and all who come after them.*

*May you each learn to create
in the pattern of the Creator.*

ACKNOWLEDGMENTS

M Y BEAUTIFUL AND gracious Audrey, who supported my unorthodox thinking over thirty years of marriage and who, in recent times, has put up with my staring into a computer screen for hours on end as I wrote this book.

To you, my dear, I owe a very deep debt of gratitude. You are all that Proverbs 31 envisions. Indeed, "You surpass them all."

To my sister Beverly and my daughter Georgia who did the preliminary edits for this book and offered helpful advice.

To the professional Charisma Media team of Allen Quain, Berta Coleman, and Ann Stoner, and to my editor, Stephanie Arena, a heartfelt thank you for all your gracious input and assistance.

I can't begin to name all those who have walked this path with me or had a role in directing and redirecting the journey that brought about this book. For fear of leaving someone out, I will stop here in naming names. But be assured my friends and extended family are dear to me, especially those who have given an ear or added their thoughts and experiences as this unusual excursion transpired.

To each and every person who had a hand in making this book possible: thank you!

THE PRAYER

Father in Heaven:

Individuals exist in every nation on the earth who deep in their being long to be a blessing to their family, their community, their nation, and their world.

Please grant that the concepts expressed in this book are understood to be of great value for the creation of stable political and economic climates. In turn, allow these scattered people to be the blessing You have called them to be.

May your kingdom come on earth as it is in heaven, for yours is the power and the glory and the kingdom forever.

Amen.

CONTENTS

PART THREE

CONCLUSION

Foreword
KNOW the TIME

From antiquity, man's fascination with time has been demonstrated in the remarkable archaeology still visible at places like Stonehenge, the flat-topped pyramids in South America, or Newgrange in Ireland. The sun, moon, and stars seemed alive to ancient man, and he came up with stories, legends, gods, and religions based on his imagination and his view of the changing sky.

Today, we have a calendar that adds one day to the next in a rising numerical progression. We still pay attention to the changing seasons as we count through the twelve months of the year. The term *month* has a connection to the lunar cycle even though our months no longer consult the phases of the moon. We do, however, look carefully at the rotation of the Earth around the sun, and our calendar is designed to closely monitor the annual cycle.

As each year ends, we add a digit to our yearly count; a practice that was arbitrarily started over two thousand years ago. Another practice that affects our measurement of time is the twenty-four-hour times sixty-minute day. This base of sixty mathematical system has been used in one form or another since Babylonian and Egyptian times. Therefore, what we have today is a breakdown of three extraterrestrial cycles for the purpose of measuring time.

First, the rotation of the Earth equals a day, which we arbitrarily broke down to twenty-four sixty-minute hours. Second, the rotation of the moon around the Earth, which takes twenty-nine to thirty days, we arbitrarily broke into months and then solidified them in the annual calendar, which is based on the third extraterrestrial cycle we use to determine time, the annual cycle of the Earth around the sun. We view the annual cycle as the most important cycle since it affects our seasons of planting and harvest. (This idea apparently has its origins in the Greco/Roman period.) All of this has a certain logic to it and is normal to us. In our part of the world, much of North America, corn is planted in April or May and harvested in September or October. The sun's angle on the Earth on May 1 is very similar, year after year, thus giving confidence that a warm spell in late April or early May should mean that frost is over for this growing season and planting should proceed.

The fact that the time element of a single day is broken down as it is also has a logic: high noon, or twelve o'clock, should mean the sun is directly overhead and at its zenith or highest point. (Daylight Savings Time is a whole other subject.) It seems our modern sense of time is mostly affected by the sun; the Earth turning on its axis gives us our days, and its rotation around the sun gives us our years. Our modern months are a nod to the old lunar calendar, but we rarely connect the phase of the moon to any element of time that affects our lives.

This leaves one mysterious element of time in our modern lives: the seven-day week. While all the other elements of time have clear connection to some celestial rotation, the seven-day week has no anchor in an extraterrestrial cycle. Follow me for a moment—60 seconds times 60 minutes times 24 hours makes a complete day; 365 days make a complete year. (Of course, every four years we have to add a day for leap year to keep things on track.) Even our months, though not tied specifically to the moon's cycle, are set up to range from twenty-eight to thirty-one days, at least closely resembling the old lunar moon.

But a week hinges on what? How did "week" come to be and what is its story? How did a seven-day time element become so important having no celestial support?

This is a study of those seven days; how they came to be, and how a little imaginative use of them can improve your life and change our world.

The story goes that a young man was kidnapped by his jealous brothers and sold into slavery. More than twenty years later, those same brothers stood in front of him begging for food and worried for their lives. Joseph's story has a key element, not of seven days, but seven years; in fact, two sets of seven years. One set of seven fat years and one set of seven lean years. Interestingly, this story, found in the first book of the Hebrew Bible, seems to echo some elements of the seven-day Creation story found in the very beginning of the Hebrew Scriptures. It would be difficult indeed to divorce our modern practice of a seven-day week from that well-known writing, Genesis chapter one.

But if Joseph's story implies value to seven years, could it be that there is significance not only for the seven-day week which we practice to this day, but for seven years? Indeed, the foundational biblical text known as the five Books of Moses includes instructions for not only seven days, but also seven months and seven years, and also seven sets of seven years; in other words, forty-nine years, to which one additional year is added to create a fifty-year Jubilee cycle.

Absolutely none of these segments of time has any obvious connection to the celestial cycles of the sun, the moon, or the stars. There is no obvious sign in the sky when these sevens begin or end. For many, it is a question that they exist or have value at all; yet the fact is that the seven-day week endures. Could it be a sign to us that the others are out there somewhere also? Could it be that though modern man often does his best to ignore a seven-day week, its persistence in sticking around is telling us we need to consider the other sets of seven laid out in the ancient texts?

What did Joseph know? Was he just lucky? Is it just a story? Even if it is just a story, what was the storyteller trying to communicate? Is it any more unusual to contemplate old words or stories and what they mean than to ponder old structures or archaeology findings and what they tell us about our ancestors?

The Books of Moses are unique in many ways, but in their use of a variety of seven segments of time, the Hebrew Bible stands alone and seems to beg us to explore its unusual ways.

Author's Note
WHY SEPTEMBER 29, 2015?

W E HAVE CHOSEN September 29, 2015, as the official release date for *Know the Time, Change your World* because of the significance of the seventh-year Feast of Ingathering in ancient Israel. Hopefully many will get their hands on the book before that date; nonetheless, there is a purposeful, grace-filled reason for the official release date.

According to the Hillel calendar, the 29th of September 2015 is the second day of the eight-day Feast of Ingathering, also known as the Feast of Tabernacles, Feast of Booths, or in the Hebrew, Sukkot. While the Hillel calendar has its detractors, it is widely accepted as the modern standard for calculation of Hebrew/biblical dates. As we will demonstrate in the book, we believe that the fall of 2015 is the end of a seventh year.

The reason for choosing a day early in the Feast of Tabernacles at the end of the seventh year is multifold. The Fall Ingathering is one of three annual pilgrimage festivals. In ancient Israel, all males were to spend eight days in a national autumn thanksgiving meeting as described by Exodus 23 and Leviticus 23. These eight days would have certainly been a time of conversations about enterprise around the country and sharing new ideas.

The Feast of Tabernacles in the seventh year had even more events prescribed. Deuteronomy 31:10 tells us that the writings of Moses were to be read to the people during this gathering (a once-every-seven-years event) and that this was the moment when all debts were to be canceled (also a once-every-seven-years event).

Therefore, we have chosen September 29, 2015, the second day of the Feast of Tabernacles, in the hope that we can share these ideas from the ancient wisdom in the moment of time when the ancient nation was to gather and Moses's writings were to be heard by the people, and when all debts were to be canceled. In other words, this was the moment of learning from God and others. It was also a time of economic reset.

If the fall of 2015 is the end of the seventh year, then it is also the beginning of a new set of seven years; this date, then, is the most gracious time to explain these ideas to this generation, as we now have seven years before the next specified cancelation of debts in the fall of 2022. Our purpose is to bring as many people into the wisdom of this calendar as possible. The hope is that many will take risks and work hard early in the upcoming seven years, with a plan to have shed that risk by the fall of 2022.

Ultimately our purpose is that many would have the resources to be more generous and join Abraham's calling to be a blessing to our world.

These things will make more sense to you after you have read the book.

I hope you have the TIME of your life!

| 46 | 47 | 48 | 49 | 50 | 1 | 2 | 3 | 4 | 5 |

Part
ONE

Chapter 1
BIBLE, BUSINESS, LIFE

MOST BOOKS BASED on biblical themes speak very little about the business world or the marketplace. Likewise, most books written about the modern world's marketplace speak very little about the Bible. A few business coach types clearly use biblical themes and even cite the Bible once in a while; but for the most part, these two—the Bible and business—are held to be different streams of life, if not simply incompatible.

The problem for me is that these two, the Bible and the marketplace, are my passion. I enjoy both deeply, and together they enrich my life and give it meaning. One without the other would fall flat, for it is in the marketplace where I can best apply biblical principles, and it is in the Bible where I learn how the marketplace actually works.

This book is the result of my getting up every workday and being responsible for employees' paychecks, vendors' bills, and customers' needs for more than a quarter century. In those years I have seen good times and bad, made great decisions and not-so-great decisions. I have had the privilege of teaching adult Bible fellowship classes at my place of worship, in my home, and in other house groups.

Theologically my roots are Anabaptist, Protestant, but my current worldview has been greatly affected by the successful establishment of the modern nation of Israel. The other huge input that has moved my thinking is the literature that has come out of Messianic Judaism and the

1

Hebrew Roots Movement during the last forty years. That said, my desire is to serve all believers with this message. My hope is to show results that may lead others to modify the way they read the Bible. It is important to emphasize here that while I love to dig for the truth, grace and mercy are always a first consideration. The reason why will become clear as the book develops.

The question I will attempt to answer is, how can the biblical record better inform our actions in the marketplace, and how can we affect the marketplace for justice, mercy, and faith? In other words, Can the marketplace be redeemed from a place of serving Darwinism to a place of loving God and serving our fellow man?

Many believers seem to have no problem with the marketplace being dog eat dog, survival of the fittest. What they see is that competition yields better service, better products, and improved life for the majority. Meanwhile, another group of believers cries out for social justice and howls about the rich abusing the poor.

Those of us from the business community tend to side more with the first group, but we must admit that the social justice Christians have the Old Testament prophets like Amos and Micah on their side. The fact is, they clearly have James, from the New Testament, on their side also.

Does this mean that faith in the marketplace needs to be socialistic, or even communist somehow? I do not think so; but maybe this is why the Bible and business rarely end up in the same dialog. Surely competition is good and inspires better craftsmanship and product, but surely caring for others is also part of our calling as believers.

So how do we walk this fine line? What are the patterns that enable us to create great products that improve mankind's lot in life without violating the biblical moral code?

We are not the first generation to struggle with keeping

a strong middle class. Wealth naturally flows to those who already have it. To counter this natural flow, we in the West have done much to improve the lives of all citizens by using a progressive bracketed income tax system. We have supported public education for all, public highways, antitrust laws, publicly funded old age pensions, health care—and the list goes on. All of these have the purpose of supporting the middle class against poverty and oppression.

Depending on who you talk to, these initiatives have enjoyed varying degrees of success; yet our world seems to cry out for a better answer. The middle class is increasingly stressed, while again wealth seems to flow to those who already have it. The problem seems to have its roots in the credit market.

Debt is the method by which middle class people buy homes, automobiles, and higher education for their children. When the economy is growing and work is plentiful, wages can pay off these debts and allow recent have-nots to accumulate equity and enter the middle class world. Western governments have also subsidized credit markets in hopes of creating growth in home ownership and education. Transportation is subsidized via public transit in the cities and public highways throughout the countryside. Auto manufacturers themselves often offer low interest rate loans for the purchase of new cars.

For many decades this borrowing to buy as a way of forced saving had a positive effect on the net worth of middle class families. Especially during times of inflation, a family with a low interest rate on their home loan could pay back their lender with dollars of lower value, while their home equity continued to increase. Loans for higher education increased the earning power of the individual, allowing those loans to be paid off easily. And since transportation was key to this earning power, most new college graduates bought cars shortly after graduating, if not before.

Because these things worked so well, home loans grew to thirty-year maturities, with some lenders loaning as much as 125 percent of value against homes, believing that homes always increase in value. Auto loans grew in maturities also, some reaching seven years, and loans for higher education grew seemingly without limit in an almost religious belief that education improved earning power.

Then, as if we were playing musical chairs, the music stopped. Overnight, credit froze. No one could borrow, as the lenders themselves had been found to be insolvent. Governments scrambled to save the financial system. Plenty has been written about the economy since the fall of 2008, and much of it mirrors what was written about previous marketplace disruptions of decades and centuries long past and conveniently forgotten.

But of all the pundits who spilled myriads of pixels on the Internet and other mediums on the subject of the Great Recession, almost no one inquired if we had violated some biblical principle. Even those who did indicate that biblical principles had been violated did so in unhelpful ways, providing lots of judgmental attitude about debt but little guidance for future hope.

Into this world of confusion and sadness, Deuteronomy 15:1–6 speaks:

> At the end of every seven years you shall grant a remission of debts. This is the manner of remission: every creditor shall release what he has loaned to his neighbor; he shall not exact it of his neighbor and his brother, because the LORD's remission has been proclaimed. From a foreigner you may exact it, but your hand shall release whatever of yours is with your

brother. However, there will be no poor among you, since the LORD will surely bless you in the land which the LORD your God is giving you as an inheritance to possess, if only you listen obediently to the voice of the LORD your God, to observe carefully all this commandment which I am commanding you today. For the LORD your God will bless you as He has promised you, and you will lend to many nations, but you will not borrow; and you will rule over many nations, but they will not rule over you.

This passage clearly limits debt to seven years—and not just any seven years. By studying Deuteronomy 15:1–6 in conjunction with Deuteronomy 31:10, it becomes clear that the biblical ideal is a complete credit cycle reset on a specific date in the fall of the seventh year:

Then Moses commanded them, saying, "At the end of every seven years, at the time of the year of remission of debts, at the Feast of Booths."
—DEUTERONOMY 31:10

The Feast of Booths, or Sukkoth, always falls in our September/October time frame. Imagine a society in which all debt is zeroed out on a specific autumn date every seven years. This is not to be a surprise event, but a designed, planned-for, built-into-the-society event.

Leviticus 25 and other passages also give us considerable information about how ancient Israel was to handle the sabbatical year. Not only were debts to be canceled, but the land was to be left untilled and slaves were to be set free. In the seventh set of seven years, an additional year was added to create a fifty-year Jubilee during which the land was transferred back to the original owners' families.

Clearly these biblical ideas are not going to be implemented as law in our Western culture anytime soon. Nonetheless, we can look for ways to improve our lives with this information. For these old economic ideas to have value, we will have to dig deep and allow our minds to wander outside modern norms. Here is where pondering the ancient documents has something to offer us.

So in essence this book will mix Bible, Christianity, and Hebraic/Jewish thinking, along with my years as a small businessman and a student of the marketplace. This book's focus will be on improving lives by adapting biblical principles and concepts to our modern walk of faith.

Along the way I expect I will stumble into a theological quarrel. Some will be tempted to argue with the words they find here; those who do are missing the point. The challenge should be to argue with the results these ideas can bring about in normal people's lives.

Chapter 2
FREEDOM vs. SLAVERY

THE FIVE BOOKS of Moses—Genesis, Exodus, Leviticus, Numbers, and Deuteronomy—are core documents of the Hebrew Bible. In traditional theological circles, it is generally accepted that these five books were written by Moses after God gave His people the Ten Commandments in the third month of the year they from escaped slavery in Egypt. The Hebrew word most often used for this section of the Bible is *Torah*, which literally means instruction or to hit the mark.

While much of the content of these books is historical stories written with a teaching purpose, some is simple instruction for how the community is to function.

When considering any section of the Torah, one needs to keep in mind that this is a document written to train slaves to be free people, in a social order. Since they had been slaves for four hundred years, Moses would have needed to use simple, direct language in his communication. Much of the writing in the Torah is written in the imperative. To our modern ears, many of the instructions seem harsh, even at times cruel. We read of stoning and persons being cut off from the assembly for violating one instruction or another and we imagine an unpleasant lifestyle, until we realize that when coming out of slavery, people are often not able to make wise choices in areas where they never had a choice before they were set free. Clearly, Moses's intent is for this group of former slaves to live as a community of free people.

He also understood that for this to happen, individuals would need to follow instructions that built up the community. They needed to grow and prosper in areas of military, diplomacy, health, economics, demographics—and most importantly, justice, mercy, and faith.

Consider the Psalms, a remarkable ancient collection of the inner thoughts of David and others who were of great influence in their time. Their love of this ancient wisdom is evident, and their meditation on it and encouragement of others to do the same is one of their often repeated themes. Psalms is the place of refuge for the troubled soul; we all turn there in those difficult times. One passage from Psalms that truly stands out is the Mem segment of the largest acrostic in the Bible:

> O how I love Your [Torah]! It is my meditation all the day. Your commandments make me wiser than my enemies, for they are ever mine. I have more insight than all my teachers, for Your testimonies are my meditation. I understand more than the aged, because I have observed Your precepts. I have restrained my feet from every evil way, that I may keep Your word. I have not turned aside from Your ordinances, for You Yourself have taught me. How sweet are Your words to my taste! Yes, sweeter than honey to my mouth! From Your precepts I get understanding; therefore I hate every false way.
> —PSALM 119:97–104

The idea that a man or woman of faith can turn to the Torah for wisdom and understanding beyond human ability is, indeed, a great promise and hope.

All the great teachers of the Torah, including Jesus of Nazareth, tell us that the most important commandments are to love God and love your fellow man. When questioned about the Torah and its most important instruction, the Nazarene gave a very insightful answer:

> "YOU SHALL LOVE THE LORD YOUR GOD WITH ALL YOUR HEART, AND WITH ALL YOUR SOUL, AND WITH ALL YOUR MIND." This is the great and foremost commandment. The second is like it, "YOU SHALL LOVE YOUR NEIGHBOR AS YOURSELF." On these two commandments depend the whole Law and the Prophets.
> —MATTHEW 22:37–40

In describing all of the instruction of the Hebrew Bible as depending on love of God and love of fellow man, Jesus is putting context to Moses's writings. While we may see something we read there as cruel or unpleasant, for a people emerging from slavery, these difficult things should be seen as tough love; or, better put, maybe difficult for the individual, but beneficial for the community as a whole.

This does, however, leave us moderns with a bit of a dilemma: what to do with instructions from the Torah that our society has not implemented. The answer must be that we adapt biblical instruction to our lives as best we can, recognizing that Scripture is perfect but we and our life circumstances are not.

Here is another of Jesus's instructions that helps us know where to put our effort. In a confrontation with the religious leaders of His time only days before his death, He tells them that some parts of the Torah are more important than others, while at the same time holding all to be valuable:

> For you tithe mint and dill and cummin, and have neglected the weightier provisions of the law: justice and mercy and faithfulness; but these are the things you should have done without neglecting the others.
> —MATTHEW 23:23

This exchange clearly demonstrates that the biggest concerns of biblical instruction are justice, mercy, and faith. To the extent that we can bring these three concepts into our lives and our society we will be an asset to our communities and honor our God and His Word.

A sad history exists among the people of God. At times these instructions, intended to set people free, are misused to put people into bondage. At times powerful or pious individuals manipulate the weak for their own purposes.

In the Sermon on the Mount, Jesus gives hope to the common man with a seemingly impossible statement:

> For I say to you that unless your righteousness surpasses that of the scribes and Pharisees, you will not enter the kingdom of heaven.
>
> —MATTHEW 5:20

To tell the common folk that their righteousness must exceed that of their religious leaders would at first impression lead the average soul to ask the question, "What hope is there for me?" However, what Jesus was announcing was the impossibility of being good enough for God by our own works or deeds. In doing so, He was encouraging each of us to look to Him for righteousness. He in turn would teach each of us how to live as free men.

On one occasion He brought a whip to the temple:

> And Jesus entered the temple and drove out all those who were buying and selling in the temple, and overturned the tables of the money changers and the seats of those who were selling doves. And He said to them, "It is written, 'MY HOUSE SHALL BE CALLED A HOUSE OF PRAYER'; but you are making it a ROBBERS' DEN.'"
>
> —MATTHEW 21:12–13

In His quest to set people free, Jesus would not abide money changers preying on the people as their hearts were being drawn to worship God. Turning the worship of God into a money making proposition was, for Him, an abomination. Worship of the true God is to be uninhibited. Woe to anyone who sets up roadblocks or tollbooths on the pathway of those who wish to worship the God of Creation.

Two biblical stories come to mind when considering how to live in a fallen world, the stories of Daniel and Joseph. Both men found themselves captive in foreign lands, yet they rose to respected leadership positions. Daniel not only was a respected advisor for more than one generation of Babylonian kings, but he was even able to keep his respectable position when Babylon fell and the Medes and the Persians took over. This type of wisdom, knowledge, and understanding is a direct result of his relationship with his God and his study of the revealed Word of God.

Daniel clearly mourned his exile, and the difficulties of his youth were never far from his mind, but he continued to believe his life had purpose. He put his energy into honoring God in the situation in which he found himself, never giving up on life and a future for his people.

Daniel's story clearly demonstrates a man who meditated and pondered God's Word, and looked for ways to apply it in his situation.

The first psalm recorded carries this theme so well that it is beloved by many around the world, with good reason:

> How blessed is the man who does not walk in the counsel of the wicked, nor stand in the path of sinners, nor sit in the seat of scoffers! But his delight is in the [Torah] of the LORD, and in His [Torah] he meditates day and night. He will be like a tree firmly planted by streams of water, which yields its fruit in its season and its leaf does not wither; and in whatever

he does, he prospers. The wicked are not so, but they are like chaff which the wind drives away. Therefore the wicked will not stand in the judgment, nor sinners in the assembly of the righteous. For the LORD knows the way of the righteous, but the way of the wicked will perish.

Notice the freedom from expectations in this psalm. The promise is that the one who meditates on the Scriptures will be like a tree that "yields its fruit in its season." On this basis, who can judge you and what you have accomplished in life?

No one! For they are not your Maker, neither do they know for what purpose you were made. Here is a promise to all who have others putting expectations on them. If you meditate on God's Word, you will produce in your time. Wait for it, in faith, and ignore the expectations of others.

Another psalm encourages us with the power of rest:

> Do not fret because of evildoers, be not envious toward wrongdoers. For they will wither quickly like the grass and fade like the green herb. Trust in the LORD and do good; dwell in the land and cultivate faithfulness. Delight yourself in the LORD; and He will give you the desires of your heart. Commit your way to the LORD, trust also in Him, and He will do it. He will bring forth your righteousness as the light and your judgment as the noonday.
>
> Rest in the LORD and wait patiently for Him; do not fret because of him who prospers in his way, because of the man who carries out wicked schemes. Cease from anger and forsake wrath; do not fret; it leads only to evildoing. For evildoers will be cut off, but those who wait for the LORD, they will inherit the land. Yet a little while and the wicked man will be no more; and you will look carefully for his place and he will not be

there. But the humble will inherit the land and will delight themselves in abundant prosperity.

—PSALM 37:1–11

"Rest in the LORD and wait patiently for Him," verse 7 begins. Only free men rest. However, look at verse 11; is it not counterintuitive that rest will lead to "abundant prosperity"? What is going on here? How does rest lead to abundant prosperity? What about all the proverbs about slothfulness? Is not work a virtue? What is the biblical view of freedom? How can we live in this freedom properly?

Joseph's life is also a great example of these concepts put into action in a foreign land. We will review his story in detail in the last third of the book, but first we will look carefully at the core purpose of our existence.

Chapter 3

A BLESSING to the NATIONS

THE BOOK OF Genesis begins to follow Abram and his descendants in Chapter 11. They become the carriers of God's plan on the earth with this remarkable promise:

> Now the LORD said to Abram, "Go forth from your country, and from your relatives and from your father's house, to the land which I will show you; and I will make you a great nation, and I will bless you, and make your name great; and so you shall be a blessing; and I will bless those who bless you, and the one who curses you I will curse. And in you all the families of the earth will be blessed."
>
> —GENESIS 12:1–3

The focus is not only on the land that God will give to Abraham, but also on the fact that He will bless and protect him. God promises to bless those who bless Abraham and curse those who curse him. For many these are just words or one more Bible verse, but the implication of this promise is profound.

Think about this promise of blessing and cursing in the context of history and many generations. One family line, Abraham's, is great and will be a blessing; others will bless him and they themselves will be blessed. Meanwhile some unwise people will curse. Those who curse Abraham, God says He will curse. The long-term consequences have many implications. First, Abraham's children should always be known for being a blessing. They can even continue to be a blessing when they are cursed, because it is God who provides for them blessing and promises that He will do the cursing to those who mistreat Abraham's children. The writer of Deuteronomy explained it this way:

> Vengeance is Mine, and retribution, in due time their foot will slip; for the day of their calamity is near, and the impending things are hastening upon them. For the LORD will vindicate His people...I will render vengeance on My adversaries, and I will repay those who hate Me....Rejoice, O nations, with His people; for He will avenge the blood of His servants, and will render vengeance on His adversaries, and will atone for His land and His people.
> —DEUTERONOMY 32:35, 41, 43

Thus Jesus's instructions to bless those who curse you in Matthew:

> You have heard that it was said, "You shall love your neighbor and hate your enemy." But I say to you, love your enemies, bless those who curse you, do good to those who hate you, and pray for those who spitefully use you and persecute you, that you may be sons of your Father in heaven."
> —MATTHEW 5:43–45, NKJV

So if Abraham's children are a blessing, the result has to be that Abraham and his descendants, and those who bless Abraham's descendants, grow in influence and numbers, while those who curse Abraham's descendants simply shrink away slowly and almost imperceptibly as the curse takes hold. Few under this curse, I suspect, ever realize why they are so "unlucky." Also, Abraham's descendants are often not aware of the consequences of their actions. When they fail at their charge to be a blessing, it seems the cursing enemy becomes strengthened and at times gains the upper hand.

This is also true when the child of Abraham interacts with other children of Abraham. Even in this situation, a child of Abraham is called to be a blessing. Failing to do so can have serious consequences, as we will see was the case in Jacob's family when we dig into their story later.

Ultimately, the believer who has been blessed with Abraham must attempt to put himself in a position of returning good for evil, while seeing to it that he does not appease evil. This is a difficult and narrow path each of us must learn to walk in our relationships with our fellow man.

David seemed a master of these two almost contradictory ideas. He was able to carefully walk this narrow path on his way to the kingship he was anointed to serve.

Consider his response to Goliath's cursing as he explained it to King Saul:

> Your servant has killed both the lion and the bear; and this uncircumcised Philistine will be like one of them, since he has taunted the armies of the living God.
>
> —1 SAMUEL 17:36

David had no doubt that Goliath had opened himself up to destruction by the words of his mouth. In his view, because he had taunted the armies of the living God, Goliath was on borrowed time.

When the two met in the field, David heard just what he wanted to hear from the giant. The Philistine said to David:

> "Am I a dog, that you come to me with sticks?" And the Philistine cursed David by his gods. The Philistine also said to David, "Come to me, and I will give your flesh to the birds of the sky and the beasts of the field."
>
> —1 SAMUEL 17:43–44

For the Philistine to curse David by his gods was a perfect way of releasing David from his obligation to be a blessing. At this point, if David had tried to be kind to the giant, the tyrant would have destroyed him; therefore, David had a confident, unyielding response, first verbal and then physical:

> Then David said to the Philistine, "You come to me with a sword, a spear, and a javelin, but I come to you in the name of the LORD of hosts, the God of the armies of Israel, whom you have taunted. This day the LORD will deliver you up into my hands, and I will strike you down and remove your head from you. And I will give the dead bodies of the army of the Philistines this day to the birds of the sky and the wild beasts of the earth, that all the earth may know that there is a God in Israel, and that all this assembly may know that the LORD does not deliver by sword or by spear; for the battle is the LORD's and He will give you into our hands."
>
> —1 SAMUEL 17:45–47

Everyone knows the story of David and Goliath. It is an often repeated analogy to sporting events or political races where an unknown, little guy knocks off the big guy.

However, the really important part of the story is mostly lost on modern leaders. Neville Chamberlain tried to appease Germany's tyrannical Hitler. It did not work then; it never works for any length of time.

That said, David handled his conflicts with his King Saul very differently. Recognizing Saul as a sovereign placed over him by God, David blessed and did not curse Saul. But it is noteworthy to observe that he also gave Saul lots of space, and did not appease or follow all of Saul's wishes once he understood Saul's intent to harm him.

The call on Abraham's children to be a blessing is more complicated and difficult than one might first reason. It is a high calling and often open to second-guessing. Not everyone who curses you is doing so as openly as Goliath did when he faced David in battle. Saul hid his cursing of David for some time. David needed to be wise to avoid being ambushed by Saul.

Jonathan thought David was wrong about his father's motivation until the two of them agreed on a test, which proved that Saul wanted David dead:

> So David said to Jonathan, "Behold, tomorrow is the new moon, and I ought to sit down to eat with the king. But let me go, that I may hide myself in the field until the third evening. If your father misses me at all, then say, 'David earnestly asked leave of me to run to Bethlehem his city, because it is the yearly sacrifice there for the whole family.' If he says, 'It is good,' your servant will be safe; but if he is very angry, know that he has decided on evil."
>
> —1 SAMUEL 20:5–7

So this test was agreed upon. Notice how the story plays out. We will come back to this story later in the book:

> So David hid in the field; and when the new moon came, the king sat down to eat food. The king sat on his seat as usual, the seat by the wall; then Jonathan rose up and Abner sat down by Saul's side, but David's place was empty. Nevertheless Saul did not speak anything that day, for he thought, "It is an accident, he is not clean, surely he is not clean." It came about the next day, the second day of the new moon, that David's place was empty; so Saul said to Jonathan his son, "Why has the son of Jesse not come to the meal, either yesterday or today?" Jonathan then answered

Saul, "David earnestly asked leave of me to go to Bethlehem, for he said, 'Please let me go, since our family has a sacrifice in the city, and my brother has commanded me to attend. And now, if I have found favor in your sight, please let me get away that I may see my brothers.' For this reason he has not come to the king's table."

Then Saul's anger burned against Jonathan and he said to him, "You son of a perverse, rebellious woman! Do I not know that you are choosing the son of Jesse to your own shame and to the shame of your mother's nakedness? For as long as the son of Jesse lives on the earth, neither you nor your kingdom will be established. Therefore now, send and bring him to me, for he must surely die." But Jonathan answered Saul his father and said to him, "Why should he be put to death? What has he done?" Then Saul hurled his spear at him to strike him down; so Jonathan knew that his father had decided to put David to death. Then Jonathan arose from the table in fierce anger, and did not eat food on the second day of the new moon, for he was grieved over David because his father had dishonored him.

—1 SAMUEL 20:24–34

Notice the significance of the new moon in this story. David wished to be a blessing, but he sensed that he was under a curse from King Saul. It seems that he used the events of a new moon gathering to test the situation. Is this just like any other gathering, or is there something significant about revelation at a new moon? Consider this: the first light of day always reveals what happened overnight. The light of day one in the Creation story was not from the sun, moon, or stars. The light of day one was divine, revealing the chaos into which the Creator would begin to work by adding to and dividing the elements, leading to new life.

David and his friend Jonathan were also using the divine revelation moment of the first light of the new moon in an attempt to reveal a matter. Indeed, just like in the Creation story, multiple divisions were going to be necessary in order to bring about the new life God had planned for David.

There is also significance to the fact that Saul waited to let his true feelings show until day two of the festival. We will explore each day of the Creation story in detail later. Suffice it to say, it makes perfect sense why Saul exploded on day two after holding his peace on day one.

My point in all this is simply that we need to try to live at peace with all men and be the blessing we are called to be, but when an individual or a group shows itself as our enemy, we have the tools of time at our disposal to reveal the hearts of men. If the divine light reveals them to be our unrepentant enemy, then we hand them over to the God of the promise, seeking direction daily for our lives. Maybe we simply give our enemies lots of space; maybe we get involved directly. Either way, we do not appease, because our greatest desire is always to be a blessing to all mankind.

Chapter 4

NATURAL RHYTHMS vs. REVELATION KNOWLEDGE

THE BIBLICAL CREATION story tells us the sun, moon, and stars were created on day four, while light itself appeared on day one. This is not at all how we experience our natural world. Without the sun, moon, and stars, our world is dark. What is going on here?

It seems to me that the writer is telling us that there is much more to light than the sun, moon, and stars. In fact, the entire Creation story has an element of revelation knowledge. The writer uses familiar natural elements to form his story, often using these familiar elements in an unusual, specific, nonlinear way.

Certainly it is unusual to think of light being four steps ahead of the sun. However, not everything about the order of things in the Creation story is beyond our experience.

Consider the first three days of the Creation story. On day one, light is called into being, showing the chaos of water over the whole globe. The writer also makes note of the dividing of or the separating of light from darkness. This separation or division becomes a theme as the story continues, and during each of the days of Creation, a separation or division takes place. The Creation process appears to be a series of additions and divisions rather than just a series of additions as we might expect.

One has a sense that light placed on the chaos of water

does little to improve the current circumstance; however, in the light, all is revealed and nothing is hidden.

Another division occurs on day two, again with little apparent positive effect on the current situation. The writer records that an expanse or emptiness was created, with some water below and some waters above the emptiness. That emptiness, we can presume, became an atmosphere (or air, as we know it), with water below being our seas, rivers, and lakes, and the waters above being our clouds.

Then on day three, the waters below gathered into one place, and dry ground appeared. In other words, again a division takes place as land appears and water is separated to a place away from dry land.

Now a logic every gardener understands takes hold. With water, light, air, and bare ground in place, plant life simply bursts out. No mystery here, no surprise; it is just as you would expect. Therefore, the process to create this perfect setting for plant life is revelatory. In other words, the events of day one, day two, and the early part of day three are additions and separations. These additions and separations are outside of our experience, while the actual sprouting of vegetation is exactly what we have come to expect.

The advent of vegetation gives us a sense of a world we understand. It is logical; we have seen it before; we even have some understanding of how it works. The journey of days one, two, and three is now behind us, and we understand its purpose.

Is this not exactly how the events of a believer's life unfold? Many times along the way, as unexpected things are added to our lives, we question if the Creator knows what He is doing, but in time we understand completely.

Have not all of us experienced this pattern in our lives? We have all gone through things that seem a total mess, additions and separations that hurt, only to come out the other

end understanding what our Creator was doing, and real-
izing that the natural growth we are now seeing could not
have happened but for the recent shaking we experienced.

Interestingly, very quickly after experiencing a shaking
set of separations that turns out to have new life in it, we
revert to our natural eyes and become comfortable with
this new growing situation. We forget the pain the divisions
caused and wish for the good times to continue—and then
day four arrives and shakes our world again.

Day four is a total surprise. The story suddenly shifts; the
natural, linear logic of day three's plant life yields to day
four's time setters: the sun, moon, and stars. Why now? We
were on a roll; why change the theme? Why, after all these
improvements on earth, use day four simply to put lights in
the sky? After all, we already have light.

The point is that this is another nonlinear/revelation
moment. The writer has allowed that there is logic to the
natural world, but he wants us to know that linear logic is
limited in its ability to explain our world. He is giving us
hints or clues that will improve our understanding of our
world. Clearly, day four is very special.

The celestial beings, we are told, are put in place to mark
the *moedim*,[1] or appointed times. The sudden break from
the run up to plant life is designed to get our attention. Day
four tells us about time and timing matters, another Creation event brought about by an event of addition and then
separation. The sun, moon, and stars are added and then
used to mark out holy or set apart days, separating these
special days from normal work days. I find it helpful to
think of day four as setting standards or a foundation for
what is to come.

Day four turns out to be the start of a whole new set of
three days, and as we discussed earlier, the new set of three
days will have parallels with the first set of three days. This

new set of three will have additions and separations also, each of which will be portrayed using subjects with which we are familiar but often explained in ways we find puzzling or less than logical in the moment.

The giving of time makers in day four is followed by the mobile, biting, self-determinate life of day five in the form of fish and birds. The division of fish below from birds above leaves the observer guessing what the connection is between day four's time setters and day five's mobile biters.

As we will show in part two of this book, this is not an accident; the time setters will be of vital importance, especially when the highest forms of life arrive on day six. The sixth-day creatures are also mobile, biting, and self-determinate life.

This brings us to the logical high point of the second set of three: the creation of man. Just like the creation of plants is the logical explanation of the creations of days one, two, and three, the creation of man is the logical outcome of days four, five, and six. Allow me to explain.

In the first set of three days, after all the elements were in place and properly separated, what seems to us as a natural event took place: plant life sprang forth.

Likewise, day four saw the creation of the celestial bodies specifically for ruling the day and the night, setting standards, and marking out the appointed times. Day five has the creation of the fish and the birds. But day six has a specific event for the creation of land beings, dividing the mammals from the creepers, and then another specific event for creating man.

So where is the logic? Just like plant life is the logical expectation of water, light, air, and dry ground, so also a ruler is the logical expectation of a system of time, applied to flocks and herds of living beings who move about according to rhythms built into their DNA. The animal kingdom follows its natural instincts. Each species is different, but individuals within a species follow a fairly tight pattern of behavior that can be discovered and exploited by a ruling time keeper. This time keeper has power over the plants as well. Indeed the human, the time keeper, is given a specific stamp of approval:

> God blessed them; and God said to them, "Be fruitful and multiply, and fill the earth, and subdue it; and rule over the fish of the sea and over the birds of the sky and over every living thing that moves on the earth."
>
> —GENESIS 1:28

What tools did God give man to allow him to rule? A mind for remembering and calculation, and a timing system that could put him in the right place at the right time for hunting, gathering, and domesticating both plant life and moving creatures.

Suddenly this all makes logical sense; we can see the usefulness of the sun, moon, and stars as we master our world by the use of time. Of course, in order to be the rulers we were intended to be, we must work with the celestial time setters, whose purpose is to rule the day and the night, in conjunction with the revealed instruction. A clock is of little value if you do not know the principles of telling time.

But we are not done; it happens again.

The nonlinear dislogic of revelation kicks in again as the seventh day is declared a day of rest. Our natural worldview is challenged. What is the Creator's purpose? Would it not make sense to put the newest, highest form of creation into action? Why rest or set a Sabbath at this moment?

Days one, four, and seven seem especially nonlinear, while days three and six seem to be logical based on the events of the previous two and a half days. As I pointed out, plant life is a logical extension of the previous events; so also, the creation of man last on day six is a logical extension of ruling lights and the mobile, self-determined life now on earth. In these moments of time, the world seems to make sense.

However, the nonlinear revelation of day one's light and the separation of that light from darkness four days before the sun, moon, and stars are created is well outside of our natural experience. Day four itself seems to interrupt the natural flow of life to bring us the sun, moon, and stars as standards of time setting.

In addition, the call for a day of rest on day seven is made immediately after the creation of the human, the highest form of creation. These are all unexpected nonlinear events that give us revelation about how our world works and how we are to function in our world.

These nonlinear addition and separating moments are there to teach us how to adapt our ways to the Creator's ways. For our natural way is to put to work our greatest creation as soon as possible, but the biblical writer shows us that God has a different plan for the first day of His prized creation. We will pursue these ideas in detail in part two, but for now let us pursue our Creator's ultimate purpose for these things.

Chapter 5
LAND, SLAVERY, and DEBT

THE FIVE BOOKS of Moses give us careful instruction about certain practices to be carried out in the seventh year concerning land, slavery, and debt. In order to understand why land is to be left fallow in the seventh year, why slaves are to be freed and debt is to be canceled, one needs to consider the purpose of the Sabbath or seventh segment of time, be it a day or a year.

Jesus gave us the answer when he explained, "The Sabbath was made for man, and not man for the Sabbath" (Mark 2:27).

In other words, the day of rest was called into existence for our benefit. It was not imposed to make our lives difficult, but rather to free us or at least put us on the path to freedom. When considering the Creation story, consider this: man is made last of all creation, late in day six. Man's first day is a day of rest; therefore, it can be said that the Creator has never allowed man to earn his day of rest.

Sabbath is always a gift from the Creator, which in turn prepares human for the work he is designed to accomplish. Just as Paul wrote to the Ephesians:

> For by grace [rest] you have been saved through faith; and that not of yourselves, it is the gift of God; not as a result of works, so that no one may boast. For we are His workmanship, created in Christ Jesus for good works, which God prepared beforehand so that we would walk in them."
>
> —EPHESIANS 2:8–10

Therefore, by extension, allowing the land to lie fallow in the seventh year not only encourages man to rest, but it allows the land to rejuvenate itself, for the benefit of the next six years of crops.

Slavery existed in those days, but its application was never allowed to destroy hope for renewal. Consider the kindness and wisdom of this instruction.

> If your kinsman, a Hebrew man or woman, is sold to you, then he shall serve you six years, but in the seventh year you shall set him free. When you set him free, you shall not send him away empty-handed. You shall furnish him liberally from your flock and from your threshing floor and from your wine vat; you shall give to him as the LORD your God has blessed you. You shall remember that you were a slave in the land of Egypt, and the LORD your God redeemed you; therefore I command you this today.
>
> —DEUTERONOMY 15:12–15

A slave set free at the end of the sixth year was not to be sent out empty handed, but to a new life, as a free man in the seventh year.

Of course the focus of this book is that debt was to be forgiven, released; thereby creating an economic balance that prepares everyone in the community for a new start for the six years of free enterprise to come.

Interestingly, while clearly all shackles are off by the start of year one, everyone is aware that seven years from now these same Sabbath instructions will apply. Therefore, free markets are always tempered with the knowledge of a coming reset.

Although these ideas are thousands of years old, sadly we have no record that they have ever been used consistently. Here is how the story of Israel is summed up after the fall of Jerusalem in the very last book of the Hebrew Bible, 2 Chronicles:

> The LORD, the God of their fathers, sent word to them again and again by His messengers, because He had compassion on His people and on His dwelling place; but they continually mocked the messengers of God, despised His words and scoffed at His prophets, until the wrath of the LORD arose against His people, until there was no remedy... Those who had escaped from the sword he carried away to Babylon; and they were servants to him and to his sons until the rule of the kingdom of Persia, to fulfill the word of the LORD by the mouth of Jeremiah, until the land had enjoyed its sabbaths. All the days of its desolation it kept sabbath until seventy years were complete.
>
> —2 CHRONICLES 36:15–16, 20–21

Israel went into exile so that the land would be given the rest it had not received. This failure to rest had apparently created a situation for which "there was no remedy." Jeremiah declared seventy years of exile as the time necessary for the land to rest. Here is a possible calculation of seventy sabbatical years from 580 BC, the decade Judah is taken to Babylon going back in time

Calculating seven sabbatical years and one Jubilee every fifty years leads us to seventy years of Sabbaths divided by 8 = 8.75, which becomes the multiplier; therefore, 8.75 x 50 = 437.5, the number of years that lacked appropriate sabbatical land rest.

If you add 437 years to 580 BC, the decade of the final exile of the southern kingdom, Judah, you find out the land has not had its appropriate rest since pre-1000 BC, very likely setting Jeremiah's reset to around the time of David, or maybe even before David was king. In other words, since the Davidic kingdom is seen as the zenith of Israel's ancient kingdom, the sabbatical years may have never been kept—or if they were kept, it was not done very well.

To this day argument exists over whether the biblical Jubilee cycle is forty-nine or fifty years. This in itself tells you that these things do not have a strong history of observance. Let us briefly dig into this forty-nine versus fifty year question.

First, I suggest we take the reading of the text at face value:

> You are also to count off seven sabbaths of years for yourself, seven times seven years, so that you have the time of the seven sabbaths of years, namely, forty-nine years. You shall then sound a ram's horn abroad on the tenth day of the seventh month; on the day of atonement you shall sound a horn all through your land. You shall thus consecrate the fiftieth year and proclaim a release through the land to all its inhabitants. It shall be a jubilee for you, and each of you shall return to his own property, and each of you shall return to his family.
> —LEVITICUS 25:8–10

The simplest reading of the text points to the logical conclusion that the fiftieth year is a Jubilee, and after the Jubilee there is an apparent restart, with a new count in year one. This view is consistent with the view of the classical rabbis (those teachers of whom we have record before the Romans destroyed the temple in AD 70).

As we have already shown and will continue to show as we go on, biblical patterns repeat themselves in groupings of time—for example, seven days, seven years, and seven sets of seven years. Likewise, the fifty-year Jubilee has at least one similar pattern. No one is suggesting that we change the count spelled out in Leviticus 23 from First Fruits to

Shavuot (Pentecost) to forty-nine days; everyone agrees the count is fifty days, at which point the appointed times disconnect from each other until the first day of the seventh month. This, it seems to me, puts a stamp of something very special, outstanding about the fiftieth day. As we will see, the fiftieth day becomes an incredible critical juncture of time. Shavuot has huge significance for our story. I expect the fiftieth year to have no less significance, and fully expect that we will all find out one day that the fiftieth year stands alone as a beacon of freedom and new beginnings!

I also count Noah's story as evidence:

> Lamech lived one hundred and eighty-two years, and became the father of a son. Now he called his name Noah, saying, "This one will give us rest from our work and from the toil of our hands arising from the ground which the LORD has cursed."
> —GENESIS 5:28–29

When Noah was born, they said, "This one will give us rest." Six hundred years later, he survived the Flood!

> Now Noah was six hundred years old when the flood of water came upon the earth.
> —GENESIS 7:6

The text tells us Noah went out, onto his own land, in the six hundred and first year:

> Now it came about in the six hundred and first year, in the first month, on the first of the month, the water was dried up from the earth. Then Noah removed the covering of the ark and looked, and behold, the surface of the ground was dried up. In the second month, on the twenty-seventh day of the month, the earth was dry. Then God spoke to Noah, saying, "Go out of

the ark, you and your wife and your sons and your sons' wives with you."

—GENESIS 8:13–16

I suspect Noah was born on a Jubilee and that is why they named him Noah (which means rest) and exclaimed, "This one will give us rest." I also suspect he was in the ark during a Jubilee, six hundred years later, and went out onto his own land in the first year after the Jubilee. For all this to work, the Jubilee calendar obviously needs to be fifty years. We will pursue Noah's story in depth in Part Three.

Indeed, Ezekiel 20 gives us the sense that Sabbath keeping was never done very well. God's complaint through Ezekiel seems to reach all the way back to Egypt:

> I made Myself known to them by bringing them out of the land of Egypt…I gave them My sabbaths to be a sign between Me and them, that they might know that I am the LORD who sanctifies them. But the house of Israel rebelled against Me in the wilderness. They did not walk in My statutes and they rejected My ordinances, by which, if a man observes them, he will live; and My sabbaths they greatly profaned.
>
> —EZEKIEL 20:9, 12–13

If the Sabbatical years were not kept for more than four hundred years while Israel and Judah were in the land, then it is very unlikely that they were kept during the exile or the extremely stressful years of the returned exiles under Ezra and Nehemiah and the later occupation of the Greeks and Romans.

So if this is the case when Yeshua (Jesus) shows up on the scene, His people would have been in need of a new beginning—a reset—a Jubilee. I believe that this story from Luke has some information for us:

And He came to Nazareth, where He had been brought up; and as was His custom, He entered the synagogue on the Sabbath, and stood up to read. And the book of the prophet Isaiah was handed to Him. And He opened the book and found the place where it was written,

"THE SPIRIT OF THE LORD IS UPON ME, BECAUSE HE ANOINTED ME TO PREACH THE GOSPEL TO THE POOR. HE HAS SENT ME TO PROCLAIM RELEASE TO THE CAPTIVES, AND RECOVERY OF SIGHT TO THE BLIND, TO SET FREE THOSE WHO ARE OPPRESSED, TO PROCLAIM THE FAVORABLE YEAR OF THE LORD."

And He closed the book, gave it back to the attendant and sat down; and the eyes of all in the synagogue were fixed on Him. And He began to say to them, "Today this Scripture has been fulfilled in your hearing."

—LUKE 4:16–21

The passage Yeshua quotes is from Isaiah 61 and goes on to talk about the restoration of the land to the people of Israel. (See Isaiah 61:4 below.) This language can only be Jubilee correlated, as the return of the land is only at the fifty-year Jubilee. (See Leviticus 25.) Land does not return to its original owners in the other seventh years:

Then they will rebuild the ancient ruins, they will raise up the former devastations; and they will repair the ruined cities, the desolations of many generations.

—ISAIAH 61:4

I contend that Yeshua was re-establishing the date of Jubilee and that this event had to happen in the late AD 20s or very early AD 30s. (I expect it was the fall of AD 29.) I intend to be generous to all other points of view here, but our focus is looking for rhymes, parallels, and patterns. If the evidence leads us to another conclusion, so be it. We need to be sure that we are not trying to force round pegs in square holes. Can I prove Jesus said these things in AD 29? No. But it seems to fit what we see in the modern marketplace, which will be described later.

Interestingly, as of this moment, the modern rabbinic count is the same as what I will propose in chapter seven, until 2029–2030, at which point their count will become year one, while in contrast, I see the fall of 2029 to the fall of 2030 as a fiftieth year. As a result, from now to 2030, our counts for the sabbatical year agree. This may be a very wonderful opportunity to work together to restore *Shmita*, the release of the seventh year.

Chapter 6

TIME and WEALTH

THE MODERN BUSINESS world does all it can to master time—or maybe, better said, to ignore the Creator's time settings. Retail establishments are increasingly open twenty-four hours a day, seven days a week, and three hundred sixty-five days per year. The rhythms of the business week, month, and year are still in place, but one can feel the pace speeding up as invoices are being sent electronically only hours—and in some cases, minutes—after a service is delivered. Technology has, in some respects, freed us by providing information at our fingertips whenever we desire. However, it also appears that large amounts of power, wealth, and control have been acquired by those who seem to have mastered the financial world by use of technology.

This is not a conspiracy theory or a finger pointing; it is simply a fact that wealth now moves around the world at the speed of light as a result of modern communication. It does so all the time. It crosses government borders, makes currency exchanges, and verifies credit capabilities, all in the blink of an eye.

Today, the marketplace rarely slows down and is never completely closed. Business models are designed to grow linearly; only in the agricultural market do seasons matter and an awareness of new beginnings exist. Even in agriculture we now have a world market, linked electronically at ever-increasing speed. Therefore, the produce of the northern and southern hemispheres, along with varying growing seasons due to the distance to the equator in each growing zone, gives us a harvest somewhere in the world at almost any time of the year.

Business schools, business books, and the pundits in all the world's centers of commerce, have only one mantra: grow! Grow your business, grow your output, grow your top line, and grow your bottom line; no matter what, a healthy business is always growing. For the most part, this also means that business is always using debt in an ever-increasing amount. Since interest on debt is a cost of doing business and therefore an expense, which is calculated just as you would calculate any other expense, the incentive to borrow is almost always high.

Into this ever-turning treadmill, Deuteronomy 15 speaks:

> At the end of every seven years you shall grant a remission of debts. This is the manner of remission: every creditor shall release what he has loaned to his neighbor; he shall not exact it of his neighbor and his brother, because the LORD's remission has been proclaimed.
> —DEUTERONOMY 15:1–2

This biblical idea is like a wrench in the spokes of the world's marketplace. It is radical, and frankly, it is not going to happen under current governing systems; nonetheless, it is God's Word. If you don't like the idea that it is God's Word, at least consider that it is a very old idea, found in the world's best-selling book.

So how do those of us who have a business calling, with employees, customers, and vendors function in a 24/7 world?

How do we who respect the Bible live our lives? How do we who have a faith that calls for periodic rest and new birth function when our culture runs contrary to these principles?

It is a challenge to be sure, and one that needs thought and prayer. Think about it this way. We still give generously with an eye toward the biblical tithe in spite of modern taxation. We still understand high interest rates to be usury and attempt to be generous when asked for a personal loan. These things being the case, we can also adapt a seven-year remission of debt to our modern hamster-wheel economy. We simply need to view the knowledge we have as revelation and then meditate and pray about how to use that revelation to be the blessing to which we were called.

Many people make the Bible difficult or more complex than it needs to be. The fact is that while deep nuances exist within the ancient text, most often a simple approach works better than a complex one, at least when starting to adapt a biblical principle to which we are unaccustomed.

Following biblical direction is usually difficult only in that it requires personal self-discipline. Think about the Ten Commandments. None of them are physically hard to follow; our failures are almost always the result of lack of discipline.

The edict of Deuteronomy 15, however, is not well known. Even when one becomes aware of the text, it is not immediately evident when this remission of debt is to take place. Furthermore, since we are, for the most part, a consumer society, we are almost all debtors rather than lenders, so our power to cancel debt is limited. However, this limitation is also power, as we can simply begin setting up our debt in such a way as to have it paid down as much as possible by the end of the seventh year.

As business people or families, we can take on risk early in the cycle of seven years and shed risk as the seventh year approaches, aggressively paying down our debts in an attempt to be deleveraged or have as little debt as possible by the end of year seven.

This simple strategy will create a number of effects. Allow me to explain. As I pointed out earlier, Sabbath was made for man. His first day was a day of rest that prepared him for the six days of work to come. The genius of being out of debt as year one starts is that the Creation story tells us day one is when the light comes on. Remember that light is not the light of the sun, moon, or stars; it is supernatural, divine light. Is it possible that we can have divine guidance for our finances?

Before I go further, let us talk about what natural man is tempted to do in year seven. Things likely went very well in year six. Remember, year six is a logical year. It makes sense to us, and things work according to the natural logic we expect. Now the revealed instruction is to rest.

In all likelihood, an enterprise has had its best year in a long time, and the opportunity seems ripe to do what every business school teaches: grow! Of course there is nothing wrong with growth, but if it requires debt (and it most likely does), then a choice needs to be made. Will I continue to work toward being de-leveraged by the end of year seven, or will I expand my operation because I think I see opportunity? Will I abandon my discipline and borrow more money in year seven?

In Deuteronomy an interesting connection is made between idol worship and the sun, moon, and stars of day four:

> Do not act corruptly and make a graven image for yourselves in the form of any figure, the likeness of male or female, the likeness of any animal that is on the earth, the likeness of any winged bird that flies in the sky, the likeness of anything that creeps on the ground, the likeness of any fish that is in the water below the earth. And beware not to lift up your eyes to heaven and see the sun and the moon and the stars,

all the host of heaven, and be drawn away and worship them and serve them.

—DEUTERONOMY 4:16–19

I believe the connection is this: worshipping the celestial beings, rather than using them to mark God's appointed
times, leads to a continuous treadmill-type religion, as these
heavenly bodies never stop; they go on and on in a continuous circle. Therefore, working continuously, not recognizing Sabbath as a gift from God that man can never earn,
puts man in a place of believing he has earned his possessions. Any man who believes he has earned his possessions
by his own merit worships the works of his hands, which
then become his idols.

Thus, these things end up being equivalent—worship of
the sun, moon, and stars; worship of idols; and living a 24/7
lifestyle, where each day is treated alike. You may need to
think about that a bit, but here is my point.

Would you not want to have your investment capital as
liquid as possible and available when the lack of rest and
the worship of idols (the works of human hands) is exposed
by the divine light? In other words, paying down your debts
in year seven rather than borrowing more to invest in the
opportunity you are sure is right in front of you is an act
of saying, "What I have is a gift from my Creator. He has
called me to rest for a year, and I am doing so by passing up
a business opportunity and following His instructions to be
out of debt as much as possible."

If the opportunity is still there in year one, then I know I
am supposed to move on it because I can see it in the divine
light. But regardless, I am not moving on it until year seven
has passed, for what I am seeing in year seven may very
well be a mirage. I have my revealed instructions and I will
rest, as instructed, as a way of saying to myself, my family,

and my God that all I have is from His gracious hand and I refuse to worship the works of my hands.

There are many nuances to the seven-year cycle, but none more profound than being ready when the light comes on in year one. The economy affects us all, but those who are responsible for businesses feel the bumps in the road in unique ways. Any business leader who has had to shrink his staff due to economic downturns knows the heartache of those meetings. Of course, the heaviest burden is on the downsized employee who goes home to his or her family without a job.

Also greatly affected is the vendor who does not get paid and the government who does not receive expected tax revenue. At times this shrinking economic climate causes multiple businesses to close due to insolvency, often affecting whole communities for generations.

So how do we adapt these ideas to our time? How do we find the end of year seven?

Chapter 7

FINDING the END of the SEVENTH YEAR

THIS STORY STARTS for me during the summer of 1991 in a Bible study with friends. That day, I heard this portion of Deuteronomy read aloud:

> At the end of every seven years you shall grant a remission of debts. This is the manner of remission: every creditor shall release what he has loaned to his neighbor; he shall not exact it of his neighbor and his brother, because the LORD's remission has been proclaimed. From a foreigner you may exact it, but your hand shall release whatever of yours is with your brother. However, there will be no poor among you, since the LORD will surely bless you in the land which the LORD your God is giving you as an inheritance to possess, if only you listen obediently to the voice of the LORD your God, to observe carefully all this commandment which I am commanding you today. For the LORD your God will bless you as He has promised you, and you will lend to many nations, but you will not borrow; and you will rule over many nations, but they will not rule over you.
>
> —DEUTERONOMY 15:1–6

I was immediately struck by the simple yet profound fact that the text called for a complete intentional collapse of the credit cycle. It became obvious to me that if a nation were to follow this concept, it would have far-reaching effects. Think about it! If all debts were canceled at the end of every seven years, would not the business community soon adapt, seeing to it that things were structured so that they held hard assets, equity, or cash at the prescribed end of the seventh year?

Which leads to the obvious question: When is the end of the seventh year?

Later that same summer day, with the help of my trusty IBM AT clone (big, clunky desktop computer for those of you under thirty), I was able to find this biblical hint:

> Then Moses commanded them, saying, "At the end of every seven years, at the time of the year of remission of debts, at the Feast of [Tabernacles]."
>
> —DEUTERONOMY 31:10

Here Deuteronomy ties the end of the seventh year, the time of remission of debt, to the biblical holiday of the Feast of Tabernacles. The Feast of Tabernacles (*Sukkot* in Hebrew) always falls in the months of September or October. Since the biblical calendar is lunar based, the observance of the appointed times spelled out in Leviticus 23 can move up to thirty days in either direction when considered from the perspective of a solar calendar such as the one we use in modern Western life.

On my mind in the week that followed that summer weekend were two dates: October 1929 and October 1987. Could it be that this pattern was still in place even though no one I knew was following it? The fall of 1929 was the beginning of the Great Depression. My grandfather had lost his farm in that era, and as a result, my grandparents lived meagerly for the rest of their lives, even in the good times.

More recently, on October 19, 1987 the stock market fell out of bed, dropping 22.6 percent in one trading day.

I know this is tortured thinking, but my first attempt at trying to understand this pattern was attempting to link October 19, 1987 ("Black Monday") to October 29, 1929 ("Black Tuesday"). When I checked the Hebrew calendar, what stuck out was that both of these events happened in the week after the Feast of Tabernacles. But I also had a problem: there are fifty-eight years between 1929 and 1987. Since the number fifty-eight is only divisible by seven if you subtract two, I obviously had two extra years to account for if I was going to tie 1929 to 1987.

In order to connect these events via the seven-year pattern described in Deuteronomy 15:1–6 and 31:10, I would have to find two additional years in the space between 1929 and 1987. Leviticus gave me a plausible answer in its description of a fiftieth-year Jubilee:

> You are also to count off seven sabbaths of years for yourself, seven times seven years, so that you have the time of the seven sabbaths of years, namely, forty-nine years. You shall then sound a ram's horn abroad on the tenth day of the seventh month; on the day of atonement you shall sound a horn all through your land. You shall thus consecrate the fiftieth year and proclaim a release through the land to all its inhabitants.
>
> —LEVITICUS 25:8–10

Now before I go any further, I want to again approach this humbly. The count or the calendar I am proposing is based on observation. It is not informed by any authority or tradition. It is simply, in my eyes, a historical, observable rhythm or rhyme.

Based on a literal reading of Leviticus 25, Deuteronomy 15:1–6, and Deuteronomy 31:10, I came to the conclusion that the fall of 1929 was the beginning of a Jubilee year. This made the fall of 1979 also the beginning of a Jubilee year, which in turn means that the present Jubilee fifty started in the fall of 1980, making the fall of 1987 the end of the first seven years of the current Jubilee fifty years.

In 1991 I had a theory that the biblical cycle had shown itself, but I needed more information on the events of 1979. I knew that era well, as I had lived through it, but even so, the details were sketchy to me. In the local library I found William Greider's book *Secrets of the Temple: How the Federal Reserve Runs the Country*. In his writing Greider details extensively the days of late summer into the fall of 1979 and shows clearly the strain on the economic system as the dollar declined in value around the world and inflation grew and grew.

At the end of chapter three, Greider recounts the events of Saturday, October 6, 1979. In a special all-day meeting, the Federal Open Market Committee made a decision to shrink the amount of money in the system, thus squeezing out inflation and strengthening the dollar. They knew this path would allow interest rates to find their own higher level.

It worked! The US dollar stabilized and inflation fell, but as some in the Federal Open Market Committee expected would happen, the economy also fell into recession as interest rates went to 21 percent, destroying many highly leveraged businesses.[1]

For the record, October 6, 1979 was the first day of Sukkot, the Feast of Tabernacles. Just like Deuteronomy said, it would have been a good time to be neither a borrower nor a lender. I now had three strong witnesses to the biblical seven and fifty-year rhythm. More would follow.

To recap, in 1991 I believed that it would be wise to be as un-leveraged as possible in the fall of the years 1994, 2001, 2008, 2015, 2022, and 2029 (with 29–30 being a Jubilee).

Almost a quarter century later, I am still open to revision of these dates, but so far they have held up very well.

In the years since, the marketplace has been amazing in its confirmation of the seven year-cycle. In each set of seven, it would have been wise to unload what was hot early in year six and be out of debt in year seven. In 1994, the disturbance was very mild; this is likely linked to the larger Jubilee cycle or to the fact that the collapse of the fall of 1987 was still on everyone's mind, keeping a lid on speculation. Certainly that lid was off by the middle of the next set of seven. Some may remember Fed Chair Alan Greenspan calling the market action "irrational exuberance." Greenspan made that remark in 1996, more than three years before the market showed any sign of weakness.

In March 2000 the Internet bubble sprang a leak. If my count is correct, then March 2000 was near the middle of the sixth year of the third set of seven years, a time to be gathering for the sabbatical year. Throughout that spring and summer, opportunities to move to safety were available as the NASDAQ (the exchange with the most new technology stocks) rallied back to prices still 25 percent higher than they had been the previous summer. By fall, however, the down trend was reconfirmed. And by the time terrorists flew our planes into the World Trade Center and the Pentagon a year later, no one doubted that the Internet bubble was over. Enron and WorldCom were shown to be frauds, and the whole economy was in a shambles.

If, as I believe, the fall of 2001 ended a seven-year cycle, then the next seven years were overwhelmed by the run-up of housing prices. In the fall of 2002, prices on homes started to move up very quickly. For the first time in recent memory, to buy a home, one often needed to offer more than the listing price. If you did not, someone else would offer more, leaving you still looking.

As the 2000s ticked by, the mortgage market seemed to be in full support of higher housing prices. Indeed, banking as a whole was very aggressive at marketing loans for almost any item, housing or otherwise. The excesses are now well known; the exact top of the housing market is thought to have occurred in early 2006, but serious declines did not happen until late summer of 2008, when the world's banking system nearly melted away, leading to some of the most non-free-enterprise actions ever taken by Western governments. The result was lower prices for not only homes, but also stocks and most consumer items. The banking crisis would have a long term de-leveraging effect, causing drag in the economy for years.

I pondered long when the best time would be to put out this book. I eventually settled on the idea of putting it out as early in the first year of the seven-year cycle as possible, which is the fall of 2015—because of the battering the main street economy took during the seven years starting in the fall of 2008, many people will need encouragement to take risk and seize opportunity in the years to come.

The one area of serious risk I see is geopolitical. Think about the Jubilee cycle and its fifty year pattern for a moment. World War I started a little more than 100 years ago in the summer of 1914, and the US Civil War ended in 1865, a little more than 150 years ago. Both these events created a dynamic shift in the economic picture. Of course, Vietnam also started to heat up around this time fifty years ago, so some of the world events we are hearing about today give me more pause than usual.

On the optimistic side, the wars and shake-ups we have seen in the Middle East in recent years make me hopeful that a new dynamic will emerge in that part of the world that could open a new chapter for freedom, justice, and economic expansion for the world.

Because 1994–2001 was a third set of seven years since the Jubilee of 1979–1980, I expect the next seven years as the sixth set of seven years to pattern after 1994–2001 in some ways. If that turns out to be the case, some of those Internet dreams may actually come to fruition. Pondering again the Jubilee pattern, in the summer of 2019 we will celebrate fifty years since man first walked on the moon. We could see some very interesting things between now and 2022.

As you can see, Deuteronomy 15 really can help you become a goal-oriented, long-term thinker.

As I suggested earlier, a simple approach that focuses on the transition from year seven to year one is a great place to start understanding this revealed instruction. To have purposefully rested in every way possible all your being, including your finances, in year seven indicates your faith in a God who gives man the Sabbath as an unearned gift. As Jesus taught an inquisitive leader of Israel, our God is always focused on providing for us new births, life from the dead, and born-again experiences:

> "Do not be amazed that I said to you, 'You must be born again.' The wind blows where it wishes and you hear the sound of it, but do not know where it comes from and where it is going; so is everyone who is born of the Spirit."
>
> Nicodemus said to Him, "How can these things be?"
> Jesus answered and said to him, "Are you the teacher of Israel and do not understand these things?"
> —JOHN 3:7–10

Dear reader, this is a spiritual journey; there is no way to predict the future or how these things may be used in your life. However, based on my experience, applying special attention to the time elements of seven, especially the times of rest, creates the opportunity for God to bring remarkable renewal into your life. The moment when the seventh segment of time turns to the first segment, and that supernatural light shows itself and reveals truth, is a moment for which to be prepared (in contrast to being tired, exhausted, or in debt, which can only lead to missed opportunity).

See the chart of a proposed modern biblical calendar at 7and5orhymes.com.

| 46 | 47 | 48 | 49 | 50 | 1 | 2 | 3 | 4 | 5 |

45									6
44									7
43									8
42									9
41									10

Part
<u>TWO</u>

40									11
39									12
38									13
37									14
36									15
35									16
34									17
33									18
32									19
31									20

| 30 | 29 | 28 | 27 | 26 | 25 | 24 | 23 | 22 | 21 |

Introduction to Part Two
The WORLD NEEDS NEW BIRTHS

IT IS WITH some hesitancy that I move beyond a discussion of the transition from year seven to year one. Without a doubt the end of the seventh year is the most profound, not-to-be-missed moment. A simple following of Deuteronomy 15 will yield untold benefit.

If you choose not to go beyond Part One in your application, I expect you will do quite well; nonetheless, the revealed instructions from the Scripture give considerably more direction and opportunity for set-apart rest and renewal brought about by divine light. The Jewish writers of the New Testament could not help but tie their teachings to Genesis 1:

> In the beginning was the Word, and the Word was with God, and the Word was God. He was in the beginning with God. All things came into being through Him, and apart from Him nothing came into being that has come into being. In Him was life, and the life was the Light of men. The Light shines in the darkness, and the darkness did not comprehend it.
>
> —JOHN 1:1–5

The writer of the Gospel of John starts his book as an echo of Genesis 1, "In the beginning." He is connecting God, the spoken Word with which God created, and the special light of day one to Jesus.

The idea that Jesus is present at the very beginning of the Creation story—that He was indeed Creator Himself—is a radical thought, but John is not alone in this thought. While John uses the language of symbols, Paul is more direct in his writings to the Colossians concerning Jesus at the Creation:

> He is the image of the invisible God, the firstborn of all creation. For by Him all things were created, both in the heavens and on earth, visible and invisible, whether thrones or dominions or rulers or authorities—all things have been created through Him and for Him. He is before all things, and in Him all things hold together.
>
> —COLOSSIANS 1:15–17

Paul goes on to explain that Jesus is first in renewal; He is the one able to restore us to our original purposes. Therefore, we as believers are new creations, having been restored to what we first were when the Word spoke us into existence:

> Then God said, "Let Us make man in Our image, according to Our likeness; and let them rule over the fish of the sea and over the birds of the sky and over the cattle and over all the earth, and over every creeping thing that creeps on the earth." God created man in His own image, in the image of God He created him; male and female He created them.
>
> —GENESIS 1:26–27

The idea that the believer in his renewed state should and will be an amazing creator himself should be no surprise. Yet it is pretty clear that we have only scratched the surface of our creative abilities. The ideas suggested in this part of the book lead us to look more closely at the Creation story and then all of Scripture in an attempt to find patterns that will allow our creative genius to thrive.

This simply cannot be an exhaustive study of all the elements of time within the Bible, but I do wish to include some highlights that stick out to me. Later, in Part Three, I attempt to flesh out Joseph's story, for I believe it holds some key insights.

Not all transitions from the seventh to the first have the same impact or effect. Clearly there are a lot of such transitions. We experience one such transition every week when at sundown on the seventh day we move to the first day. Generally speaking, these transitions happen without much fanfare or disruption.

Leviticus lays out for us a set of seven months annually, starting in the spring. In keeping with the revelation of day four from the Creation story, the writer gives us some words worth pondering:

> Speak to the sons of Israel and say to them, "The LORD's appointed times which you shall proclaim as holy convocations—My appointed times are these: For six days work may be done, but on the seventh day there is a sabbath of complete rest, a holy convocation. You shall not do any work; it is a sabbath to the LORD in all your dwellings. These are the appointed times of the LORD, holy convocations which you shall proclaim at the times appointed for them."
>
> —LEVITICUS 23:2–4

As the writer begins to explain the appointed times (*moedim*) of the seven months, he makes a point to highlight the Sabbath, which we have seen is a key timing issue.

Also notice the New American Standard uses the terms "the LORD's appointed times," "My appointed times," and "these are the appointed times." If we believers are pursuing God's timing in a matter, would it not be logical to start here?

The three pilgrimage *moedim* (appointed times) are

Passover, Shavuot (Pentecost), and Sukkot (Feast of Tabernacles). (If these biblical markers on the calendar are unfamiliar to you, plenty of literature is available today from both Jewish and Christian sources, helped greatly by the Messianic Jewish and Hebrew Roots Movement.) You will gain insight of great value in many areas of life by studying and pondering these things, and there is no better way to learn more about these appointed times than by putting them into practice in your home. Our family's favorite book on the subject is Valerie Moody's *The Feasts of Adonai, Why Christians Should Look at the Biblical Feasts.*

My point for this discussion is that all these special moments in the year are marked by the lunar cycle. The cycle of the moon is mostly ignored in Western culture, yet its value is pronounced. I highly recommend a study of Leviticus 23 and the biblical holidays to help you get in tune with God's revealed appointed times.

As we will explore in detail in Part Three of this book, Joseph is clearly sitting in prison with the revealed calendar, waiting for a chance to put it to good use.

We do not know how much of these patterns the patriarchs knew, but we can be sure that knowledge of segments of seven was in use, as it was Joseph's father, Jacob, who suggested to Laban, "I will serve you seven years for your younger daughter Rachel" (Gen. 29:18).

It appears that the patriarchs understood the sets of seven and thought of a set of seven as a whole, a unified one, a day of its own. Notice this idea in Genesis 2.

From the beginning, this pattern is set; the Genesis 1 story is detailed in its specific and different characteristics of seven separate days. Then almost immediately a second Creation story starts, but this time the text says, "This is the account of the heavens and the earth when they were created, in the day that the LORD God made earth and heaven" (Gen. 2:4).

This second telling of the Creation story lumps all of Creation into one day, immediately after having gone through the story day by day, showing a creative division for each day of six (with a seventh day for a rest, or Sabbath). In the second telling, these seven are seen as one day. In other words, a week of seven days is a unit of one; a week of seven months is a unit of one; a week of seven years is a unit of one; and in addition, a week of seven sets of seven years with a fiftieth year Jubilee is a unit of one.

I intend to focus mostly on sets of seven years for this discussion, but clearly the others are in the mix also. The Jubilee specifically, as we will see, cannot be ignored.

While a simple following of the instructions to allow land to lie fallow and remitting debt will mark compliance with Deuteronomy 15, in this section I want explore deeper, more detailed biblical information that may teach us about what to expect at different times during both the seven year sets and the fifty year Jubilee sets of years.

As a businessman and a history buff, I have found the timeframes of seven years and fifty years most helpful in decision making. As Mark Twain allegedly said, "History does not repeat itself, but it does rhyme." I have found those rhymes to be most evident when considered in increments of seven years and fifty years.

Three other writers have had a big impact on this study for me.

Thomas Cahill has a series he calls the Hinges of History. Specifically these three books—*How the Irish Saved Civilization*, *The Gifts of the Jews*, and *Desire of the Everlasting Hills*—have had a profound effect on my view of history and the social sciences. Cahill has an understanding of how ancient man thought and wrote, and he clearly recognizes that the Hebrew Bible changed many cultures for the good by teaching values of justice, mercy, and faith in a world that previously was simply ruled by strength of tyranny.

Leon R. Kass, in his book *The Beginning of Wisdom*, explores Genesis as only a professor with a philosophical bent could. He uses his experiences in the classroom pondering Genesis with his students to bring us many great insights on origins.

Jeff A. Benner is a brilliant man who works in our nation's nuclear power plants. He also writes and has done a remarkable job of uncovering the Paleo Hebrew alphabet. In doing so he has brought much new light to the ancient texts. His work can be found at www.ancient-hebrew.org. Any reference I make to the Paleo Hebrew is the result of Jeff's work.

One thing that makes this study so very hard to explain to Westerners, and maybe everyone, is that there are several sets of sevens that are running simultaneously. The largest segment of time we are working with is fifty years, which is more than half a typical lifetime. The smallest segment is a seven-day week. This means that no set of seven is alone and operating without some pull or push from a larger or smaller set of seven.

For this study I want to focus mostly on the block of seven years, because we have this excellent instruction about economic rest at the end of every seven years. We clearly also have instructions about specific appointed times during a set seven months of the year; therefore, we need to consider that those appointed times will have some effect or pull on the larger seven-year time frame.

Likewise, we also have instructions concerning seven sets of seven years, which ends up creating our fifty-year Jubilee cycle. Our focus on a specific block of seven years will also be affected by the pull of this larger segment of seven sets of seven years.

This is similar to the calculus computation of a thrown or launched projectile, which will give a calculated point of ultimate impact, as gravity will see to it that the projectile's trajectory is a predictable arc. However, breezes and thermal updrafts will have an effect on the ultimate point of impact.

Similarly, the larger and smaller cycles of seven may be thought of as wind and other atmospheric conditions, which will affect the ultimate results. These other larger and smaller sevens create a soft landing or a hard landing for the seven-year cycle depending on the arc of each of the other sevens—and, I would add, depending on how out of balance we as humans become in our worship of the idols our hands create.

How our creations land is very dependent on how well we, the creators made in the image of the Creator, are using the Creator's plan for our creations.

So as you can see, not all blocks of seven years are the same; in fact, one could argue that the only thing we know for sure is when we are supposed to rest as prescribed on the seventh.

However, a study of the smaller and the bigger sevens may help us pick better times for our launches of risk taking and enterprise while giving us a sense of the expected rhyme of each specific set of seven years.

Being out of debt at the end of year seven is a simple instruction. However, the sevens both large and small will have an effect, and have a lot to tell us.

Each set of seven is a complete unit, yet with seven distinctly separate segments of time, each having at least one distinct characteristic.

To go deeper we will need to think carefully about the revealed character of each day of creation, and using other biblical stories, attempt to learn even more about each of the time segments of seven. Once that is completed, we can begin to consider how the overlapping larger and smaller segments affect each seven-year cycle. We will need to develop eyes to see things that are not evident to those without the revealed instruction.

With some merit, the beauty in nature often draws us to a conclusion that if left alone by man, the natural world would improve. In addition, the natural world continues to provide mankind with food, clothing, energy, and ideas for improvement of our lives. Birds taught man to fly, fish taught us how to probe the ocean depths, and simple things like a seed that sticks to our clothing taught us Velcro.

The natural world regenerates itself in so many ways it is hard to even express. Each plant has a life cycle of seed, sprout, plant, flower, and back to seed; the animal kingdom follows suit with its own cycles of the generations, and so does humankind.

The observer of nature is drawn to the conclusion that these things go on and on ceaselessly. He soon realizes that all he sees is a constant circle of life. Even as he looks up, he realizes that the sun, moon, and stars are in a circle of motion without end.

The naturalist soon begins to look for ways to influence his world in order to stay warm, avoid hunger, and produce offspring of his own. His is a world on the move, and if there are gods, they must somehow connect to this constantly moving circle of life he sees all around him.

In time, he establishes a cult of worship on a high hill with a clear view of the sky, often placing markers so he can identify when a circle has been completed. He is naturally predisposed to worship powerful things he cannot control. History show us that mankind is drawn to worship things more powerful than himself, considering them to be gods. Thus, around the world, nature worship is marked by appeasement, sacrifice, and when the desire seems to be stronger than the effect, moves on to unspeakable and horrific acts.

Into this world of the naturalist, Deuteronomy speaks to Israel of another way:

> So watch yourselves carefully, since you did not see any form on the day the LORD spoke to you at Horeb from the midst of the fire, so that you do not act corruptly and make a graven image for yourselves in the form of any figure, the likeness of male or female, the likeness of any animal that is on the earth, the likeness of any winged bird that flies in the sky, the likeness of anything that creeps on the ground, the likeness of any fish that is in the water below the earth. And beware not to lift up your eyes to heaven and see the sun and the moon and the stars, all the host of heaven, and be drawn away and worship them and serve them, those which the LORD your God has allotted to all the peoples under the whole heaven. But the LORD has taken you and brought you out of the iron furnace, from Egypt, to be a people for His own possession, as today.
>
> —DEUTERONOMY 4:15–20

The biblical writer has two warnings: do not make images of anything (obviously a warning against idol worship), and do not worship the celestial bodies (the sun, moon, and stars).

For many years I have watched the arguments over the Genesis Creation story with some amusement and some sadness. The traditional argument of creationism versus naturalist-evolution, seems to produce considerable heat, but not much light.

The Evolutionists are the modern cousins of the worshippers of the sun, moon, and stars, and many Creationists are locked in a circle of their own as they exhaust themselves trying to out-argue the Evolutionists. As we will see, a true Creationist is a rest-first believer who understands that the Creation story is the foundational truth about how the world works.

Of course Genesis explains how the world was made, but it also explains how the world continues to be made, reshaped, and molded by the very creature God said He made in His image—us.

According to the biblical model expressed in Genesis and clarified further in the other books of the Bible, segments of seven are put into our instruction for living as not only seven days, as in one week, but also seven weeks, as in the count up to Shavuot/Pentecost, and seven months, starting in the spring month of Nissan and concluding with the fall month of Tishrei, as explained in Leviticus 23. There are two more: the sabbatical seven-year cycle; and seven sets of seven years plus one year, which ends up being the Jubilee cycle—both of which are outlined in Leviticus 25.

All these sets of seven are given to mankind, the being created in the image of God, so that he also can create.

Our Creator has given us all the tools we need to show the naturalist-evolutionist that creation definitely happens in sets of sevens. And since we are created in the Creator's image, we can, should, and must create using His pattern. To do so we need to ponder the divine revelation and also discipline ourselves to follow the divine revelation.

None of this is so difficult; our biggest problem is that we often fail in two areas. One, we fail to meditate on what the instruction means; and secondarily, even when we know its meaning, we fail to discipline ourselves to follow through on the revelation, because our natural eyes are often telling us untruths.

The biblical calendar can be used to teach us when to trust our instincts and when to hold our natural inclinations in check. The crowd or the majority is not always right, nor is it always wrong. Anyone who is always in the majority will often be wrongly swept along. Likewise, anyone who is always swimming upstream will be exhausted, as well as wrong, much of the time.

The key ingredient of successful creation is to not always be with the flow or always be against the flow, but to have some sense of when to enjoy movement and save the energy by being with the flow and when to stand alone on principle, expending energy and taking risk. The text shows us that much of the time our natural eyes do not understand what is going on, but once in a while our natural vision is to provide the next step or direction. Knowing how to discern the moment is of great benefit for our creative calling.

This part of the book is set up to encourage creation by us, the created in God's image, by following His methods of creation. Each day of the Genesis 1 creation has characteristics that can and should be applied to all the other segments of seven as well. The other sets of seven also have instructions, which can further help us understand each segment of the seven as unique and set apart.

As you continue to read, and I write of these sets of seven, I often use the word *day*. However, keep in mind that *day* could be applied to any of the biblical segments of seven. Also remember that our main focus is sets of seven years, which seems to be the longest amount of time we humans as creators can focus on a goal and not lose heart.

To discredit the Evolutionist dogma, a believer functioning as a creator will need to consider the revelations of Genesis, which inform us that every day has a different purpose. To live in this lifestyle will require thought, awareness, and discipline.

However, of all the things that I would like to convey to my readers as they start this second part of the book, none is more important than this thought: Mankind is God's special creation, made in His image. He wants to have a relationship with His special creation and to teach us His creation style.

My approach to these things is a result of my calling and experiences in a particular place and time. Your life is likely completely different, yet I expect if you can learn to use time in the same manner as our Creator did in Genesis 1, your creative skills will amaze even you.

As you learn to wait for the divine light of day one, you will have supernatural clarity for your creative gifts. Further, as you learn the purpose of each day, you will begin to understand the role of setbacks and nonlinear events in your life that will provide you with the ability to be steadfast and stable as you guide your creation, whatever it is, to its completion.

> Be transformed by the renewing of your mind.
>
> —ROMANS 12:2b

As you enter this mind-set, you will find yourself rejoicing in the role for which you were made: creator in the image of our Creator. You will also find that as you learn the seven segments of time, you will be put in multiple places to experience new birth over and over again. And you will be reminded of this profoundly concise explanation of the *Light* of day one.

> He is the image of the invisible God, the firstborn of all creation. For by Him all things were created, both in the heavens and on earth, visible and invisible, whether thrones or dominions or rulers or authorities—all things have been created through

Him and for Him. He is before all things, and in Him
all things hold together.

—COLOSSIANS 1:15–17

You have my permission to stop now and just follow Deuteronomy 15; by doing so you will do just fine. If you plan
to keep reading, put your thinking cap on—you are going
to need it.

Chapter 8

REST IS FIRST

D AY SEVEN: OUR first day was a day of rest.

God created humankind in his image, in the image of God did he create it, male and female did he create them...

Now God saw all that he had made, and here: it was exceedingly good! There was setting, there was dawning: the sixth day.

Thus were finished the heavens and the earth, with all of their array.

God had finished, on the seventh day, his work that he had made, and then he ceased, on the seventh day from all his work that he had made.

—GENESIS 1:27, 31–2:2,
SCHOCKEN

The linchpin of all biblical timing models is this one thought: "Rest is first!"

For the purposes of this book, the Creation story of Genesis 1 is vital information. Read it and meditate on it until the following two paragraphs become familiar to you. These are the patterns we will see over and over as we progress through the details that follow.

The Creation story opens with darkness, wind, and water, and, in revealed progression, adds light on day one to separate darkness from light. The separation of upper water from lower water to create space for life or air in day two, and the separation of dry land from water on day three, both lead to plant life last on day three.

This seems to complete a cycle, as the sun, moon, and stars created in day four echo the light of day one. Thus begins a new set of three, with day five's birds and fish echoing the separation of lower from upper water, and the creation of space in day two, and day six's mammals, creepers, and man echoing the dry land and new life of day three.

Thus we have the writer's view of a perfect six days of creation, but a big change has now happened for all weeks to come.

Humanity was the last creation on the sixth day; therefore, the human race's first full day was day seven, a day of rest, or in biblical language, Sabbath. This little thought is very helpful for understanding the biblical writer's purpose. In our natural mind-set, we attempt to earn our days off of work. Few employers would offer a vacation day before some amount of days were spent "earning" a day off. Yet, for a hunter-gatherer society, observation was the key to survival. Any work that followed was based on the plans established during observation. To just jump in and start working would have likely been a huge waste of precious energy.

Think about humankind's first twenty-four hours according to Genesis 1.

Let's say the man becomes a conscious human about 3 o'clock on a sunny afternoon. Almost as soon as his eyes adjust to the light, he becomes aware that he is not alone; creatures great and small move about on the ground, in the water, and even in the air.

Surely Adam is amazed at the creatures and the activity around him. Very soon the big, bright light begins to near the edge of the earth and soon disappears, and with it goes Adam's ability to see well. Adam's first moments in the sun lasted only a few hours, according to the biblical standard, as the sun sets and a new day begins.

For Adam this has to be a troubling development; we cannot know exactly what he felt, but we can all identify with being in an unusual place and having the lights go out. Our eyesight is our most precious sense. Without it—or even with it diminished—we feel vulnerable.

As the light wanes, little lights become evident in the sky above, and one large light gives dim light through most of the dark time. The sounds and smells are restful and peaceful.

When the bright light returns, the activity of the creatures picks up greatly. Adam spends his day walking around looking at all that is going on, wondering, "What is my role? What am I supposed to do?"

These are the underlying principles of day seven; rest is first. While Adam's so-called day of rest is the seventh day, for us it is first. Our first full day is a Sabbath. We did not earn a day of rest; it was a gift. Properly observed, it will bring about a sense of wonder and awe. It is completely appropriate to walk about and observe, and ask the question, "What is my role? What am I supposed to do? What will I put my energy into in the six days of work about to begin?"

An understanding of the seventh day can be fleshed out more completely by thinking about many other passages from the first five books of the Hebrew Bible. Taken together and mulled over, they give us a complete rundown of timing models based on time in segments of seven.

These segments of time, thought of in seven separate units, have a spiritual connection to freedom. Remember that the main focus of the first five books of the Bible is to provide instruction for a nation of former slaves to live as a cohesive society of free people. There is no better example of this than the biblical holidays.

An explanation of seven months, starting in the spring and ending with a great holiday seven months later in the fall, is found to be the annual calendar of these ancient tribes. One item that sticks out is that three times each year—twice in the spring and once at the great harvest holiday in the fall—everyone gathers in one location, some people apparently traveling many miles. When you think about it, this idea alone has the effect of keeping any dictator or strong man from hoarding power. Any leader will have to be able to stand up to a gathering of the people three times per year:

> Three times a year you shall celebrate a feast to Me. You shall observe the Feast of Unleavened Bread; for seven days you are to eat unleavened bread, as I commanded you, at the appointed time in the month Abib, for in it you came out of Egypt. And none shall appear before Me empty-handed. Also you shall observe the Feast of the Harvest of the first fruits of your labors from what you sow in the field; also the Feast of the Ingathering at the end of the year when you gather in the fruit of your labors from the field. Three times a year all your males shall appear before the Lord GOD.
> —EXODUS 23:14–17

The events of the seventh month, including the Feast of Ingathering (which is another name for Feast of Tabernacles or Sukkoth), are of importance as we explore the seventh segment of time, or seventh day.

Leviticus 23 is one place these seven months are explained and details for the annual calendar are set out. The seventh month, reminiscent of the seventh day of Creation, is given special attention. The first day of the month is a day for blowing trumpets—a call to wake up, be aware, and prepare yourself by making things right with your fellow man.

On the tenth of the month is a solemn assembly, a Day of Atonement, a day to consider that you have flaws and need supernatural help to live this life. It was a historical moment when sacrifices were offered for the sins of the whole nation. It is the most solemn day on the whole annual calendar.

There is one more observance, the Feast of Tabernacles, beginning on the fifteenth day and lasting eight days. These are the happiest days of the Hebrew year. During these eight days, the nation was instructed to gather at the appointed place of worship, live outdoors in temporary shelters, and celebrate the harvest and God dwelling among man.

Now we need to look at this seventh month, particularly in the seventh year. In the seventh year, the Israelites were not to plant their land, but to live on food stored up from the previous year and what grew up on its own. This has echoes of Adam walking around in wonder and awe. I expect this was a year of lots of new ideas. As the observer of this instruction would not work in the fields, he had time to tinker with an idea or a brainstorm he may have had during the last six years. Surely this would have been an innovative society.

At the end of the seventh year, the people were to release or forgive debts; in the fiftieth year, they were to return land to the family to whom it was originally assigned. These are economic resets that modern economies have no ability to mimic.

One can only imagine the joy these events would provide for the beneficiary if everyone understood that a debt only lasted until the end of the seventh year and the land would return to the original family at the Jubilee. The whole community could and would rejoice, even those who were giving up the balance on a debt due them or a piece of land, for they knew and had planned for this day just as the beneficiaries had. The grantors of these returns would have been seen by the community as kind and gracious, which has its own benefits for mind and spirit.

Interestingly, Tishrei, the seventh month of the biblical calendar, is also the first month of the new civil year, which logically starts in the fall. Why logically? Because just as man's first day is a day of rest, so also a biblical year starts in the fall and winter—in the same manner, rest is first.

The biblical calendar is broken down into potentially two sets of seven moons. The autumn month of Tishrei is the first month on any Hebrew calendar. It is also the seventh month of the summer seven-month cycle, which starts with Nissan, the month in which Passover is held, as Exodus 12 explains.

Now, of course we know that our modern calendar year has only twelve months. Even if one month is counted twice as both the first and the seventh, the calendar still only has thirteen months—one set of seven and one set of six months. This is true most years. However, because the biblical calendar puts more emphasis on the lunar cycle than on the solar cycle, every few years a month must be added to put the annual cycle, or the rotation of the earth around the sun, in cohesion with Nissan being a spring month. Otherwise, in time, Nissan would be in the winter. Therefore, just as the modern calendar adds a leap year every four years, the Hebrew calendar, in keeping to a strict lunar calendar of twenty-nine or thirty days, adds a leap month called Adar 2 every two or three years. In the years with an Adar 2, the Hebrew calendar is literally set up as two seven-month segments, a winter and a summer segment, with the fall month of Tishrei serving as both the seventh month of the summer set of seven months and the first month of the winter set of seven months.

This concept of two sets of seven months in a year may be one of the most challenging concepts for us moderns to process. It takes some time to allow your thinking to adapt to it. It is helpful to understand that the purpose of breaking these elements of time into sets of seven (or in this case, at times, less than seven) is to always have the resets— or "God's red lights," as I like to call them—spaced in such a way that risk of collapse or exhaustion is minimized.

The winter and the summer sets of seven months can each equal one, and can stand alone. However, together, the winter and summer sets of seven months represent one year, and for our purposes completely parallel day one of the Creation story.

Just as the writer declares:

> God separated the light from the darkness. God called the light day, and the darkness He called night. And there was evening and there was morning, one day.
>
> —GENESIS 1:4–5

Winter and summer are a direct parallel to the biblical separation of day and night: "There was evening and there was morning, one day."

So where does this leave us? Modern society has built a system that runs twenty-four hours a day, seven days a week, year round. Some have suggested that modern society is breaking God's law; I suggest, rather, that modern society is breaking itself. Many are losing their freedom due to non-observance of these divinely revealed concepts. I suggest that these concepts are still available to be grasped by the average person, who is seeking freedom, and will put his or her mind and actions into a plan that lines up with this system of sevens.

These ancient ideas found their way into the world's most influential book, the Bible, a book with roots going back thousands of years. The record is sketchy as to how these things were practiced. We know for sure that they were often ignored, just as they are today, at times resulting in different consequences.

Keep in mind that since we were created in God's image, our creative style is likely similar to His. In the next six chapters, I will review each day of the Genesis 1 Creation story, adding timing elements from other sections of the Bible as well in an attempt to give the reader a sense of the core revealed creation process.

Rest indeed is first. In the next chapter, we will explore what happens when we fail to rest in day seven. Ultimately, we will return again to the seventh day in chapter 14. These times of prescribed rest are truly the safety boundaries of our work.

Chapter 9

The TRANSITION FROM SEVEN to ONE

Light on Chaos

The earth was formless and void, and darkness was
over the surface of the deep, and the Spirit of God was
moving over the surface of the waters.

—GENESIS 1:2

THE SECOND VERSE of Genesis 1 describes the earth
before the seven-day week, and in particular the Sabbath. In my view, it will also eventually be our situation if
we don't follow day seven instructions. The clearly defined
events of the six days of work have brought order, but failure
to follow the instructions for day seven will bring about
degeneration and return us to the chaos of verse two. The
prescribed antidote is to pull back and disengage from the
normal work of our hands on day seven.

Again the instructions for day seven are different from
the instructions for month seven, which are also different
from the instructions for the seventh year and for the seventh set of seven years, or the Jubilee. However, in each case
a shift away from what had been during the previous six
is evident, and the pattern holds regardless of which set of
sevens we are discussing. This brings me to the words of
Genesis 1 verse 5.

God called the light day, and the darkness He called
night. And there was evening and there was morning,
one day.

This may be the first example of the concept that for us,
rest is first, before work. As I pointed out in the previous
chapter, the seventh day was man's first day, since he was
created last on day six. His first full day was a day of rest
during which he could observe and ponder all of creation
around him and consider what he would do in the six days
of work that followed. Likewise, on the very first day the
Creator separated light from darkness and set evening as
the beginning of the day, therefore setting darkness—and
by implication, rest and sleep—before morning light and
work, again showing rest before work. This shows clearly
that rest is not to be earned, but is a gift that was given at
the very beginning of man's existence to prepare us for our
purposeful activities or works.

By the time Adam is made, much order has been brought
to the chaos found at the beginning of the Creation story. If
Adam rests properly, he should find things stable and functioning well when he rises on day one to begin his six days
of work that God has prepared for him.

This may explain why the first letter of the Hebrew
alphabet is the *aleph* and its original character was the
head of an ox, which means strong, power, or leader. These
ideas of strong new beginnings can certainly be the case if
one enters day one well rested with a strong vision for the
six days to come. We actually see a strong beginning rather
than a weak beginning. How is that possible?

Look again at Genesis 1:5; the last two words are "one
day," or in the Hebrew, *yom echad*. *Yom* is the Hebrew word
for "day," but the use of *echad*[1] seems to be giving us some

guidance. It should be noted that *echad* is used here rather than the word *ri'shown*[2].

Ri'shown is used in the below passage to indicate that Esau was born first:

> Now the first [Ri'shown] came forth red, all over like a hairy garment; and they named him Esau.
>
> —GENESIS 25:25

Ri'shown clearly is the word for first in line, but *echad* has a different sense to it. While it is also used in many cases as "one" or "first," *echad* also has a characteristic of unity or harmony. Here is a good example from Chronicles:

> All these, being men of war who could draw up in battle formation, came to Hebron with a perfect heart to make David king over all Israel; and all the rest also of Israel were of one [echad] mind to make David king.
>
> —1 CHRONICLES 12:38

This verse demonstrates the harmony factor of echad. There were obviously many minds, but all agreed or were in unity (echad). Therefore, by using *echad* rather than *ri'shown*, the Genesis writer is showing us that while indeed the day of light is the first day, there is also a unity factor. I suspect this tells us that what happens on day one, or year one (or whichever sequence of seven you are studying), has a unity or harmony with the other six that will follow.

Thinking expansively, day one *yom echad* seems similar to a fertilized egg growing to its completed gestation by the end of day six. If this is the case, then greatest attention needs to be given to the events and characteristics of day one. For what we observe in the divine light of day one will likely have some unity with what we will experience throughout this particular set of seven.

This unity is a source of strength when combined with stored energy from Sabbath. The Creation story is telling us something further, and that is what happens when man, a created being with the abilities to exercise self-determination, to communicate, and to consume and destroy makes the wrong choices and instead of resting on a day seven chooses to go his own way. This causes chaos and destruction, and brings weakness rather than strength into the light of day one.

Here is where the Creation story begins to explain God's dealing with man's failures. The failure to rest as prescribed on the seventh day is a clear indication that man is more impressed with the works of his hands than he is with God's work. He has six days to work in the world God created and to follow his God-given, self-determined dreams; but on day seven he is called to lay down his self-determination and to rest. He is not given a lot of instruction about what it means to rest, or exactly what he should or should not do, but he is not to do what he has done for the last six days! He is to stop and rest. For many of us there is nothing harder than laying down our self-determination.

So what can we expect on day one? Well, day one's most common theme is evil brought to light. Those who fail to rest, who continue to work because they worship the works of their hands rather than the Creator Himself, create chaos, and find themselves and their evil exposed when the divine light comes on in day one. Therefore, the Creation story offers us a choice: rest on God's appointed time, or work 24/7 and find ourselves and the chaos we created exposed for all to see.

One more thought: the Jewish writers of the New Testament clearly saw that the light of day one was not the result of the sun, since the sun was not created until day four. In many ways and in many places they tell us they believed that the *Light* of *yom echad* was Yeshua (Jesus), none more so than John at the beginning of his Gospel. Consider his rhythm and flow compared to Genesis 1:

> In the beginning was the Word, and the Word was with God, and the Word was God. He was in the beginning with God. All things came into being through Him, and apart from Him nothing came into being that has come into being. In Him was life, and the life was the Light of men. The Light shines in the darkness, and the darkness did not comprehend it.
>
> —JOHN 1:1–5

Following the instructions for the seventh day as a way of preparing for the Light of day echad is much more than a business strategy. To be prepared for the Light of the World, "full of grace and truth" (John 1:14), is a profound opportunity we should not miss.

Ours is a fallen world, and there is no doubt that some will attempt in every weekly cycle to work straight through the seventh day; therefore, even if you choose to rest you may be affected by the chaos others create. But your awareness of the rest appointed for the seventh day will give you time to ponder and be prepared for the six days of work that start on day one. Therefore, when the light comes on in day one, at least you will be rested, and hopefully you will have a vision for the six new days of work about to begin.

As you wade into the new week, the key is to not be surprised at the degree of chaos, but to be prepared, having worked through the previous week and rested in the Sabbath as prescribed by our Creator. We need not be overwhelmed by the circumstances but we can be prepared to live out our purpose to be a blessing to the nations, fulfilling Abraham's calling. We should learn the secrets of each day of the seven-day week and apply them not only to days but also to months, years, and seven sets of seven years.

In day one the light comes on and we can see the mess that has been created. As we move on to day two, things don't necessarily get better quickly. As we will see, the energy stored up in day seven will be needed before order can be restored. Rest before work sticks out as a uniquely gracious pattern of time management.

This gives us a clue why debt and the use of credit needs to be minimized at the end of the seventh year. Having our finances in balance as we begin a new six years of work makes sense, just like getting a good night's sleep before a big day. But there is one more significant thought I want to pass along at this juncture.

I have come to believe, and observation has taught me, that the wisdom of the instruction concerning year seven has a lot to do with the events of the following year one. The single characteristic of day one in the Creation story is the advent of *light*, and so it has been my observation that the instructions for year seven are simply to prepare you for that startling moment when the *light* comes on in year one. Our resources and energy should be at their highest point of flexibility and vigor as we begin the new six years of work.

Working inside this pattern will not allow you to predict the future, but it will get you ready for the future six days of work—and especially the *light* of day one! This pattern will protect you from the Jeff Skillings and Ken Lays of Enron 2001, and the Bernie Madoffs and Bear Stearnses of 2008.

As we will see, we are given special instructions to be extra generous in year three. I can't think of anything more terrifying than to arrive at year one tightfistedly or with a secret idol. I humbly submit that the real reason for Sabbath is so we do not worship the works of our hands. If we do worship the works of our hands, we can expect the LIGHT of *yom echad* to expose it to the world.

Chapter 10

DAY TWO TAKES a TOLL

Day Two: Separation of Waters

God said: Let there be a dome amid the waters, And
let it separate waters from waters!

—GENESIS 1:6,
SCHOCKEN

DAY ONE SIMPLY put light on the chaos. In day two,
improvement begins. But even with the light on, few
consider the events of day two as an improvement; opti-
mism is in short supply.

Day two gives you a feeling that the chaos is continuing,
only now with the light of day one revealing it in all its
lack of order. Yet as we continue on in the Genesis account,
it becomes clear that the shaking of day two is purposeful
and a sign of the order to come. Space is being created
for future life. Water, a symbol for chaos, is being separated into two areas—above and below—and a new space
between them is created. "An expanse in the midst of the
waters," verse 6 says.

Now this is very troubling, especially for the naturalist
who barely survived the transition from day seven to day
one. The duress of the near escape, followed by the sight of
the destruction in day one and then another shaking in day
two, often leads a person to give up and lose faith just at the

crucial moment, even though the shaking of day two creates a space that will ultimately support life.

Remember in 1 Samuel 20 when King Saul was able to hold his peace about David on day one of the New Moon celebration, but day two got the best of him, exposing his true feelings about David even though he did not want them exposed.

This phenomenon is also well described in the stories of the Book of Numbers. Numbers recounts the events of year two in the wilderness. It is true that there were many trials and struggles in year one, as described thoroughly in Exodus; but in year one, the Israelites were given the Torah on Mount Sinai, and the survival of their escape was fresh in their minds. Year two, however, seemed to wear on the people's patience in a whole new way. Many rebellions are described throughout the Book of Numbers.

For a time even Miriam and Aaron lost their willingness to follow their brother Moses, which is recorded in Numbers 12. Then at the peak of the growing season, twelve spies are sent into the Promised Land to bring back a report. Keep in mind that timewise they are now within a few short months of year three. As we will see, wonderful things happen in day three—but the people of Israel cannot hold on to the dream any longer. When the spies report of wonderful things but great dangers, the people simply hear the "but" of great dangers. They can no longer deal with the stress; they want a fix now. They are unwilling to go through the shaking needed to prepare them for the gift they are about to inherit.

It is my firm conviction that God intended to take them into the land in the third year. Caleb and Joshua knew it, and that is why they tore their clothes. They recognized that all they had been through, all the preparation that difficult times had produced, was about to be lost right on the doorstep of the Promised Land. Interestingly, the others soon recognized their mistake, but could not recover the lost years. So it was that, sadly, forty years would pass until a new generation could move forward with the dream.

In my experience, year two is often difficult. It has a grinding effect, especially for a leader who is trying to guide a people to a new paradigm. A stiff upper lip and firm faith are the only tools. And if Moses, Joshua, and Caleb failed to persuade their congregation to follow, what are our chances?

But the fact remains, the shaking of day two creates space for life. One needs to know what time it is in order to not lose hope as the space for the new life to come is being prepared.

First Corinthians 10:6 says that all these things were done as an example for us. Their example gives us hope and the ability to stay on task so that we can keep our courage as we build toward day three, fully prepared for the next amazing phase.

The message of the Book of Numbers is that failure to let the pressures of year two form us into what we are to become will produce subpar living for a long time. Knowing that you are living in a year two goes a long way toward giving you the ability to have the correct attitude.

Day two seems as chaotic as the events before day one. However, amid all the shaking, with water above and water below, suddenly a space develops or opens up in the middle of the chaos. A space for what?

We know it is a space for life, but without knowledge of the fact that it is day two and good things are coming, that space very well may seem like cold air when you come out of the water. The fact that this opening is space for life is not evident via natural observation, but we have the revealed knowledge that life will come. Those unaware of the revealed count have no idea what the space means. To them it just seems like more confusion.

Here is an interesting thought: In Hebrew, the alphabet is also a means of counting. The second letter of the Hebrew alphabet is *beyt*, which literally means "house." In its original Paleo form, the letter was the floor plan of a two-room house or tent. A house or a tent is a space for life.

Knowing that it is day two can be very helpful in keeping your chin up and your plan on track. It also can give you the courage to step into a space that opens up, while others are still convinced that chaos is the only order of the day. The second segment of time in our set of seven is a time of continued testing. It has openings or space for future life, but you must have the means and be willing to step in when the water is still swirling above and below.

Another analogy is that of a planted seed. The first step is to plant; the second step is the decaying of the outer coating of the seed; before the third step, when the germ of life springs forth. Some breakdown is still happening in day two. It is a messy time. But our instructions are to remain steadfast, doing our part, working to help things move in the right direction.

To review, the *light* of day one has revealed chaos, and it also has given us hints about this new set of seven. As I showed earlier, the Genesis writer's use of *echad* gives us some indication that day one has in it all the elements of, or has unity with, the six days of work to come. With this in mind, we watch day one intently for clues about the six days of work to come. As evening comes and the beginning of day two approaches, we need to prepare ourselves for the natural feeling that we are headed back to the chaos in the dark of Genesis 1:2. There is simply no sign in the natural elements that gives any hope of improvement.

Indeed, as I pointed out above, even the full and complete

work of day two has no hopeful signs in it for a natural observer, unless he or she is aware of the revealed, which is that there will be space for life created amidst the chaos of water above and the chaos of water below.

This is a good time to point out a few fundamentals. Those who are aware of the revealed times are working from a different reality. As Deuteronomy explains, this reality gives direction for decision making that is unavailable to the uninformed.

> The hidden things are for YHWH our God, but the revealed-things are for us and for our children, for the ages, to observe all the words of this instruction.
> —DEUTERONOMY 29:29,
> SCHOCKEN

Certainly science and academics, in their study of the natural world, have done wonders for mankind, increasing our life spans and improving our health. But one has to wonder if certain things are hidden from the observer of nature. Keep this thought in mind as we move along, commenting on these segments of seven and the transitions. The instruction to work will be there when the natural feeling is that it is useless, and the temptation to work will be there when the instruction to rest is given.

So what is asked of us on days one and two is that with steady faith we work to improve the current condition without regard for how we feel. This is a moment when we need to look for even the slightest hint or direction from either the light of day one or an opening of space in day two.

Now we can see the great importance of day seven and the gift of rest on that day. To enter day one strong as an ox, one must have used day seven as a time to rest and strengthen in every way possible. In a practical sense, a large debt load at the end of day seven will likely be an unbearable burden and certainly will hinder taking advantage of new light and space in days one and two.

Being prepared for days one and two is crucial, resource-wise, but also emotionally, as few others will see what you are seeing. Observers of nature will see and feel only chaos on days one and two. Meanwhile, we will put forth effort and resources toward faithfully improving the path barely discernible to others.

Chapter 11

YEAR THREE: AFTER a DIFFICULT START, IT ALL MAKES SENSE

Day Three, Dry Land, and New Life

> God said: Let the waters under the heavens be gathered to one place, And let dry land be seen! It was so...
> God said: Let the earth sprout forth with sprouting-growth, Plants that seed forth seeds, fruit trees that yield fruit, after their kind, (and) in which is their seed upon the earth! It was so.
>
> —GENESIS 1:9, 11,
> SCHOCKEN

D AY THREE IS that amazing moment in time when water, light, air, and bare ground suddenly exist simultaneously. Water in uncontrolled, chaotic arrangement preexists day one giving us the first element necessary for life, but in destructive, overwhelming form. Days one and two had only one event or new feature each: light and the separation of darkness from light in day one, and space or air as waters were separated below and above the space in day two. In contrast, day three has two new features: bare ground as it is separated from the water below, and vegetation.

Day three has a sense of accomplishment to it. From the beginning water existed; in day one light appeared; in day two air, or space for life, was added as the waters separated.

Now in day three, dry land is seen, and very logically, vegetation appears.

I do not wish to ignore the miracle of plant life, but any gardener will tell you that the combination of water, light, air, and bare ground will yield some sort of plant life almost without trying. Thus we see that vegetation is the logical extension of the events of days one and two and the bare ground of day three.

The third letter of the Hebrew alphabet is *gimel*. Its original character was a sketch of a human foot, and it means to gather, walk, or carry. It also has ancient ties to wealth and independence. Throughout the biblical text, the third day is unique in its ability to bring us new-life surprises.

Abraham received Isaac as if back from the dead on the third day, as on the mountain of seeing (Mount Moriah) God provided a ram in place of Isaac. After some time in a fishy situation, Jonah decided that he would go to Nineveh after all when the big fish spit him up on a beach on the third day.

And of course the Man from Nazareth, in exactly the same pattern as the first Passover lamb in Egypt, died on the fourteenth of Nissan at twilight. And three days later, just as the children of Israel had walked out of Egypt to freedom on that very same day centuries earlier, He walked out of His grave, delivering mankind from the slavery of sin.

The last part of the Creation story's day three, without a doubt, is a profound shift from the previous two days. Days one and two seem chaotic, with lots of movement; and then suddenly in day three, when bare ground is separated from the water, the new life of vegetation appears.

The new life of vegetation is also the most easily managed of all the created life, for as we will see, new life created in later days of the story is much more difficult to control or put to good use. Day three is also a moment to prepare for what comes next, as day four will bring some surprises of its own.

The Creation story in many ways seems to defy the observer of nature, but in the second half of day three, things suddenly make sense to the natural eye. Water, light, air, and bare ground are followed by plant life.

If only the naturalist had done more in days one and two to prepare for the new life of day three. The point is that anyone who has worked with a plan based on the revelation given in Genesis 1 has been at work from the moment the light came on in day one. He has been able to discern a direction in which to go, and in day two found a space for life. By the time bare ground appears, he is ready and can make his rows of garden produce straight. He is also ready to pounce on the weeds he wishes to not grow.

The additions and separations that the worker within the revealed plan has experienced were not necessarily pleasant, but they were not unexpected either—this made them tolerable, since shaking and upheaval was expected.

New life on the third day is a biblical theme with which every student should be familiar. So much could be written about the third day, the third month, the third year, and the third set of seven years that we could fill up many pages.

Here are few more events connected to this third day phenomenon; this time, however, we are looking at third month events. The Ten Commandments were given to the children of Israel early in the third month of the year that they left Egypt. This event is commemorated in the biblical calendar as the Feast of Weeks, or Shavuot, and also is known in the Greek and Western world as Pentecost, *penta* due to its counting of fifty days from the Feast of First Fruits, which is during the Passover season. Of course Pentecost is when the Holy Spirit came on the early believers in Jerusalem as described in Acts 2; therefore, it is valid to say that the Holy Spirit came early in the third month as well.

Both these events are new life, rebirth events. The Torah or Law given to former slaves was to teach them how to live as free men. Prophets like Ezekiel had long predicted that God would send His Spirit to write God's instructions on His people's hearts:

> Moreover, I will give you a new heart and put a new spirit within you; and I will remove the heart of stone from your flesh and give you a heart of flesh. I will put My Spirit within you and cause you to walk in My statutes, and you will be careful to observe My ordinances.
>
> —EZEKIEL 36:26–27

Certainly both the original giving of Torah at Mount Sinai and the later outpouring of the Holy Spirit in order to write Torah on our hearts are life-from-the-dead, third-day events.

Hosea also saw a third-day experience coming. While his exact meaning is not clear, it is clear that he saw the third day as a day of new birth:

> Come, let us return to the LORD. For He has torn us, but He will heal us; He has wounded us, but He will bandage us. He will revive us after two days; He will raise us up on the third day, that we may live before Him. So let us know, let us press on to know the LORD. His going forth is as certain as the dawn; and He will come to us like the rain, like the spring rain watering the earth.
>
> —HOSEA 6:1–3

So back to our present situation.

Suffice it to say that on this third day new life of vegetation is what we have been seeking. We longed for it on day one; we longed for it on day two; and now that it is here, we need to consider what it means and how to care for it. Here at this moment in time, in the third year, we receive some special instruction about what to do with this new life that has just burst forth:

> At the end of every third year you shall bring out all the tithe of your produce in that year, and shall deposit it in your town. The Levite, because he has no portion or inheritance among you, and the alien, the orphan and the widow who are in your town, shall come and eat and be satisfied, in order that the LORD your God may bless you in all the work of your hand which you do.
> —DEUTERONOMY 14:28–29

We are instructed about a special tithe of year three. Why year three? One can only assume that because of the expectation of new life in year three, the instruction is to remind us to be extra generous at that point, remembering this newfound wealth is from God. I find it especially interesting that this instruction comes only two verses before the instruction of Deuteronomy 15:1–6 to remit debts in year seven. Both instructions seem to be saying that any wealth that has come into your hands in the years of abundance must be acknowledged as gifts from our God, and are to be shared and used to provide new beginnings for others.

In Deuteronomy 26 the same instruction is given, but a few additional instructions are added:

> When you have finished paying all the tithe of your increase in the third year, the year of tithing, then you shall give it to the Levite, to the stranger, to the orphan and to the widow, that they may eat in your towns and be satisfied. You shall say before the LORD

your God, "I have removed the sacred portion from my house, and also have given it to the Levite and the alien, the orphan and the widow, according to all Your commandments which You have commanded me; I have not transgressed or forgotten any of Your commandments. I have not eaten of it while mourning, nor have I removed any of it while I was unclean, nor offered any of it to the dead. I have listened to the voice of the LORD my God; I have done according to all that You have commanded me. Look down from Your holy habitation, from heaven, and bless Your people Israel, and the ground which You have given us, a land flowing with milk and honey, as You swore to our fathers."

—DEUTERONOMY 26:12–15

Here we are also instructed that after we have been generous, we are to bring it up in prayer to God and ask Him to bless us as a result. Do you see humility and confidence before God in this direction? It certainly seems as though the Creator takes great joy in seeing His special creation, made in His image, create using His pattern of creation. He wants us to tell Him how we are doing.

Here are a few more thoughts about the vegetation of day three. It is stationary; it is stable; it cannot move or communicate; it grows slowly; and it provides the base of the food chain for all the future life to come.

What is our role? I am reminded of the gardener who was showing his pastor around his garden. The pastor commented on how God had very much blessed the garden, to which the gardener responded "Pastor, you should have seen it when God had it alone!"

Indeed, in the second telling of Creation in Genesis 2, God's first explanation of Adam's purpose was to cultivate.

Even before his fall, Adam had a role of work, which was, first and foremost, caring for the earth.

> Then the LORD God took the man and put him into the garden of Eden to cultivate it and keep it.
> —GENESIS 2:15

We have a role; we are part of Creation. Whatever our calling, it will take both our effort and the miracles of new life for our gardens to produce well for the benefit of our families and our world.

So to the third day...*Here! Here!*

Or as Tevye sings in *Fiddler*, "To life, to life, l'chaim... L'chaim, l'chaim, to life."

But before we celebrate too much, let us look in on our friend without the revelation.

Imagine the natural observer at the end of day two. He has made one of two choices during the overwhelming disarray that has come to light: either he has given up, or he has tried to fight through to what he hopes will be better times. If he has given up, and survives, he will be in hunter-gatherer mode when the new life of day three emerges. His garden will certainly not have clean rows of valuable produce, but he may find some remnants of previous caretaking.

However, consider the naturalist who has worked through the entire period of chaos. The light of day one gives him some hope that a better day may be around the corner; however, that light fades into a long night of doubts. If his determination survives the night, the light returns on day two, renewing his hope. But alas, day two only yields some space or an opening amidst the water that still swirls above and below. Now the light fades again as day two draws to a close, and he faces what he suspects is another long night.

At this point our hard-working naturalist is in danger from

his own hand. Exhausted from the stress and doubt, as well as the physical labor, his temptations are appeasement, capitulation, and irresponsibility. Can he find within himself the strength to endure another long night, or is he so psychologically broken that he will make a self-damaging decision?

As the light dawns on day three, the doubts are huge. The real question is, can anyone endure without the revealed knowledge that there is life in day three?

How much more will an individual work hard and take chances in days one and two, and how much more cheerfully and steadfastly can a person endure day one, day two, and the early dark hours of day three, if he understands the whole revelation of the first three days of Creation?

The revealed things that belong to us and to our children teach us that we need to rest on day seven because it will be more than two days before we see that new vegetation.

No wonder Nicodemus was puzzled when Jesus told him, "You must be born again" (John 3:7). For Jesus these things were elementary, as His greatest rebuke to Nicodemus was, "Are you the teacher of Israel and do not understand these things?"

New birth, life from the dead, is foundational to biblical thought. Any religion without it is simply works of man, which can only lead to death, appeasement, and stress twenty-four hours a day, three hundred sixty-five days per year.

The biblical path to new birth is rest. It cannot be earned. It cannot be bought. It is a gift that must be accepted. You cannot simply accept new life; you must accept the gift of rest so that new life can come. Now that we have experienced new life, what comes next? Our story finally turned logical at the end of day three. Could anyone have guessed the events of day four? I doubt it.

Chapter 12

The SECOND SET of THREE

Day Four, Setting God's Appointed Times

> God said: Let there be lights in the dome of the
> heavens, to separate the day from the night, that they
> may be for signs—set times, for days and years.
>
> —GENESIS 1:14,
> SCHOCKEN

D AY FOUR IS a logical disconnect from the progression
of days one, two, and three. When considering the first
three days as a unit, they make sense. The existing water of
the original chaos, the light of day one, the created space
between the upper and lower water of day two, and the dry
land of day three understandably produce vegetation.

But what of day four? It has no relationship or connection
to the first three days except that it parallels the "let there
be light" of day one by providing light in defined forms: the
sun, moon, and stars. Therefore, day four seems to be a new
beginning. Days four, five, and six parallel their counterparts in the previous three days, but this does not mean that
they are only a repeat. Instead, they are highly enhanced
versions of their previous counterparts.

The startling transition from the new life and abundance of day three to the emptiness of day four has been
recognized for generations. The fourth letter of the Hebrew
alphabet is the *dalet*. Its original character was a symbol

representing a floppy, swinging tent door. In contrast to the third letter, *gimel*, which is associated with wealth and independence, the dalet has long been associated with weakness and poverty. It's easy to see why after the abundant new life of vegetation in day three, day four yields only lights above for signs and set times.

In many respects, day four is a return to the newly revealed chaos of day one. This causes great confusion for the untrained logical thinker. In the West, we expect each day to be added to the next and build on yesterday's accomplishments. Yet suddenly on day four the logical progression stops. A reversion to a day similar to day one takes hold, which throws many into confusion.

Day four begins a new series of three, and as such, it has more in common or "unity" with day one than it does with day three. Indeed, the transition from day three to day four can be most counterintuitive. The biblical writer is showing us these celestial bodies have two purposes, the first of which is "as signs for seasons, and for days and years." The secondary purpose, apparently, is "to give light on the earth." The writer goes on to speak of the greater light to govern the day and the lesser light to govern the night:

> Then God said, "Let there be lights in the expanse of the heavens to separate the day from the night, and let them be for signs and for seasons and for days and years; and let them be for lights in the expanse of the heavens to give light on the earth"; and it was so. God made the two great lights, the greater light to govern the day, and the lesser light to govern the night; He made the stars also. God placed them in the expanse of the heavens to give light on the earth, and to govern the day and the night, and to separate the light from

the darkness; and God saw that it was good. There
was evening and there was morning, a fourth day.
—GENESIS 1:14–19

Much more is going on here than simply providing light.
From this day forward it will be the sun and the moon that
will set time and identify appointed times to those of us
who embrace the revelation.

In contrast to the divine light that appears on day one,
the writer shows the lights in the heavens as created objects,
not eternal, brought into existence on the fourth day. In
other words, the celestial bodies have a beginning and, as
modern researchers now know, they also will have an end.
This is a very passive-aggressive way to demonstrate that
the ancient pagan practice of worship of the sun, moon, and
stars is meaningless.

We are subtly warned that these lights above are not gods,
but we are to pay attention to them. It is by their guidance,
in collaboration with the revealed instruction, that we will
be able to identify important elements of set-apart time,
including days, months, and years.

Notice the phrase "for signs for seasons" in verse 14. The
word "seasons" is the translated Hebrew word *moedim*.

Moedim is best translated as "appointment" or "appointed
time." In other words, the sun and moon will be used to
guide us to specific moments in time.

This is the purpose of our entire study: to coordinate our
efforts with the Creator's timing. But what times? you may ask.

Earlier I mentioned the biblical Feast of Tabernacles, its
significance concerning the release of debts in year seven
(according to Deuteronomy 31:10), and the role it played in
identifying this pattern.

Look again at Leviticus 23 verse 2 from the New American Standard: "The LORD's appointed times which you shall

proclaim as holy convocations—My appointed times are these." Twice in this verse the term *appointed times* is used, both clearly defined as God's appointed times (moedim).

Leviticus 23 goes on to define, by use of days and moons, many moedim, including the eight days that start on the fifteenth day of the seventh moon—the appointed time of Tabernacles. As a matter of fact, Leviticus 23 lays out its appointed times in the period of seven lunar cycles. Here is one more place to gain insight concerning the pattern of seven built into creation.

Indeed, a study of these seven moons and the appointed times in them reveals that while there is a considerable amount of appointed times during months one, two, and three, months four, five, and six are without appointed times or festivals. The implication may be that months four, five, and six are times to be industrious, hunting, gathering, and harvesting.

Another thought to ponder is that Leviticus 23 lays out seven separate appointed times and festivals. Exodus tells us that three of them are pilgrimage festivals. The instructions for these times direct all males of adult age to gather at the place of national worship:

> Three times a year you shall celebrate a feast to Me. You shall observe the Feast of Unleavened Bread; for seven days you are to eat unleavened bread, as I commanded you, at the appointed time in the month Abib, for in it you came out of Egypt. And none shall appear before Me empty-handed. Also you shall observe the Feast of the Harvest of the first fruits of your labors from what you sow in the field; also the Feast of the Ingathering at the end of the year when you gather in the fruit of your labors from the field. Three times a year all your males shall appear before the Lord GOD.
> —EXODUS 23:14–17

The pilgrimage appointment of the first month is that of Unleavened Bread, starting on the fifteenth day of the first moon of the year. Since Passover begins at twilight on the fourteenth and is to be celebrated into the night of the fifteenth, the first annual pilgrimage encompasses three appointments: Passover, the Feast of Unleavened Bread (which is a week long), and First Fruits (which falls during the week of Unleavened Bread on the day after the Sabbath).

This first pilgrimage festival is a pattern Bible students see over and over.

Three separate events join together to yield one event, leading to life from the dead. In the Exodus story, on the fourteenth day of the first month the Hebrews were still slaves. That evening, they killed a lamb and put its blood on their door frames. When morning light came on the fifteenth, the Egyptian firstborn were dead. Israel, in great haste, was separated from the Egyptians, plundering them of silver and gold. They leave so quickly, there is not even time for their bread to rise. They arrive at the Red Sea apparently on the third day. (I say apparently because the third day is not called as such; but notice the third day images.)

The newly freed Hebrews are at the Red Sea with no path ahead, only water in front of them. The Egyptians have had second thoughts about letting their slaves go free with their silver and gold. This is exactly how things looked early on the third day. Evil has been brought to light, opportunity has been seen, but a new life of freedom is still beyond reach without the separation of water and dry land. Notice the miracle is just that: a third-day event of separation of water and dry land. Notice also, once the separation of water and dry land occurs, the people themselves walk to the safety of the far shore and new life. Evil is bogged down and swept away as this new life on the other side begins. I pursue this line of thinking more in Appendix Three.

The second pilgrimage festival is Shavuot, or Pentecost, which I spoke of in the previous chapter. This appointed time is connected to the first pilgrimage festival of unleavened bread by a counting of seven weeks or fifty days from the appointed time of First Fruits. The name *First Fruits* reminds us of the third day of Creation and leads us to the conclusion that it is day three in the week of unleavened bread, the same day when the Red Sea event happened. Is that the case? I cannot prove it, but it seems logical.

Seven sets of seven days later, on the fiftieth day, Shavuot (the fourth festival) sets the standard for this new life of freedom. This is the time when the Ten Commandments were given on Mount Sinai, and it is also the time the Holy Spirit was given to believers in Acts 2 later in the first century.

These events of the third month are life-giving, as are all third days. These are also standard-setting events. Just like day four sets the standard for time, so also the fourth appointed time, Shavuot or Pentecost, is a standard-setter. The Torah and the Holy Spirit will provide direction and wisdom for living that new life.

The fact that the fourth appointed time is found in the third month seems to indicate that these new standards are going to yield an extraordinary new life of freedom. It also indicates that during moments of great increase or new life, we should focus on divine instruction.

Notice these words from Deuteronomy concerning the purpose and value of these instructions:

> See, I have set before you today life and prosperity, and death and adversity; in that I command you today to love the LORD your God, to walk in His ways and to keep His commandments and His statutes and His judgments, that you may live and multiply, and that

the LORD your God may bless you in the land where
you are entering to possess it.
—DEUTERONOMY 30:15–16

One way to get the most out of your study of the ancient
Hebrew Bible is by considering what is not said. The Hebrew
language itself is minimalistic in its function. Translators
will tell you it often takes multiple words to convey in English what Hebrew conveys in one. In addition, often what is
not said is also a message. For example, as I pointed out earlier, in the Creation story light appears on day one but the
celestial bodies of light only appear on day four. This is a
quiet dismissal of worship of the sun, moon, and stars; thus
it is important to listen to the silence.

As I observed earlier, the appointed times cease, and for
the fourth, fifth, and sixth months of the hot summer, all
is quiet on the biblical calendar. This seems to say, "You
have been given resources and freedom, and a standard
of instruction has been set; now go and see what you can
do." The fourth month is a new beginning, set up with an
exceedingly good foundation.

The expectation is that industrious people will do quite
well in months four, five, and six under these circumstances,
which will lead us to the events of month seven.

I will pick up with lessons from the fifth, sixth, and seventh appointed times when we look again at day seven in the
last chapter of this section, as all of the last three appointed
times fall in the seventh month.

Our modern calendar is designed to take us away from
the appointed times of day four. To find our Creator's
appointments and rhythms, we will need to return to a calendar governed by the sun and the moon.

The celestial lights do us no good on their own, but joined
to the biblical revelation they allow us to be in time with

the rhythms of the Creator and His creation. Used properly, they will enhance our work and our rest.

Concerning day four itself, it has no new life in it as day three does, and may feel like a useless day to the naturalist. However, it is actually a profoundly important moment, when a whole new standard is being set. Be careful, diligent, and wise on day four, as it will set the standard for many days to come. Even more importantly, ponder and act to put your life in the rhythm of the *moedim* of Leviticus 23. After all, if our Creator has appointed times with His people, I can't imagine anyone would want to miss them.

The fourth day is certainly a time to be aware, as the changes from day three are profound. It also is a time for learning to use some new tools. The meaning is clear: YHWH has appointed times, the fourth day's celestial lights are created to show us when these times are, and these times will be our tools to deal with the challenges to come.

As we move into day five, it will become evident why these appointed times are so important. There simply is no way to handle days five and six consistently without understanding our Creator's appointed times. While day four is void of new life and may seem rather boring, the upcoming events of day five may have you longing for a break, wishing you had paid more attention to the instructions concerning the appointed times.

To review, let us check in on our naturalist friend.

The transition from day three to day four is a disappointment for the naturalist thinker. We noted how everything suddenly made logical sense in day three when water, light, air, and bare ground suddenly yielded the new life of vegetation. For the naturalist, the hope is that we have turned a corner and the logical growth of our enterprise will continue. Having suffered through days one and two, he grasps the results of day three as proof of better days ahead.

In day four, however, things on earth see no improvement at all. Instead, new lights appear in the sky overhead. The naturalist has run into a day that is all about setting standards—most importantly, standards of time.

Long term, the benefits of this day will become evident for those who understand the revelation; but in the moment, day four is a confusing disappointment for anyone seeking a continuation of or improvement on the first three days. Indeed, day four is the beginning of its own set of three days. Just as the divine light of day one exposed chaos and signaled that order was about to begin, so also the lights of day four signal an opportunity to bring order to the most difficult concept of time.

The element of time in our world is a mystery. Often it is simply accepted rather than explored. It is taken for granted as ordinary rather than thought of as extraordinary. In order to harness this component of our lives, moderns have created a calendar that, using mathematical dates, simply moves forward in a steady march, adding one day to the next.

We rarely think of the celestial bodies as time-setters, and it seldom occurs to us that in some way we may have lived this day before, or that history may have clues for us based on the rhythms of the heavens. Therefore, we miss many opportunities for new beginnings and sound endings. Our transitions in life are chaotic as a result, halfhearted and often forced by circumstance.

And no wonder, since by the end of day four our natural eyes have seen one day—day three—in which new life has been evidenced. Three of the four days so far have been seemingly sterile or inert. Our patience continues to be tested. It's obvious now that days one and two were necessary for the new life of day three. But day four returns us to testing mode and requires more grit and determination. As our story develops, it will become obvious that the time setters of day four will also be of great value. We are about to experience life very unlike the life we were so happy about back in day three.

In terms of the seven-year cycle, the special tithe of year three we discussed in the last chapter is similar to the Sabbath in that it puts us again in a mode of acknowledging that what we have is from God's hand. It prepares us uniquely for year four. As we now know, year four—like year one—is a new beginning. We will need all our tools and resources in order to succeed when year five is revealed. Year four is a time to set standards and consider the times, looking back over previous cycles and setting out on a new or altered path.

Chapter 13

The LIVING CREATURES, SURPRISE and DANGER

God said: Let the water swarm with a swarm of living beings, and let fowl fly above the earth across the dome of the heavens!

—GENESIS 1:20,
SCHOCKEN

God said: Let the earth bring forth living beings after their kind, herd-animals, crawling things of the soil after their kind!

—GENESIS 1:24,
SCHOCKEN

IF DAY FOUR was too boring for you, day five will make up for it. We are about to experience new life in a very active and, at times, terrifying form. Just as day four showed some parallels to day one, so also day five parallels day two. In day two, the waters were separated above from below, with space between. In day five, two kinds of life are given: one for the water below (swimmers, or fish), and one for the space above (flyers, or birds).

A new life of swarming sea creatures and flocking air creatures fills the seas and the skies, showing clearly day five's rhyme with day two.

But these creatures are not to be taken for granted or simply admired. Unlike the plant life of day three, these creatures have very unique capabilities. They are "living beings," or in the Hebrew, *nephesh chay*.[1] This implies that along with having physical bodies designed for travel in their element—water or sky—these creatures also have mouths and teeth. They can bite, communicate with each other, and their brains enable them to exercise self-determination. They go where they wish, often at very high speeds. The plant life of day three is the base of their food chain, but they also feed on each other (and you, if they get a chance).

To survive and prosper in day five, one needs good timing. These new creatures are vastly unlike the vegetation of day three, which was immobile and could be harvested in a predictable pattern. The birds and fish of day five are a considerable challenge. Capturing them is very difficult, not to mention the fact that they eat the vegetation of day three and will bite you whenever they get a chance.

Interestingly, the new ecology is self-sustaining. In addition to the food chain, the plants produce the oxygen the birds and fish consume. In turn, the creatures produce carbon dioxide, which the plants consume. The element of time marked by the celestial bodies of day four will now become crucial for success, as any gathering of new life will require being at the right place at the right time with means and a plan.

Opportunity on day five is huge, almost unimaginable. It requires good timing and a capacity to handle some very difficult creatures, creatures who have the breath of life, minds of self-determination, and bodies of flesh that can fly or swim with strength and skill.

In keeping with the action theme, the fifth letter of the Hebrew alphabet is *hei* (pronounced "hey") and has a root meaning of action, spirit, and revelation. The four-letter name of God uses this letter twice. In addition, hei is the letter that was added to Abram and Sarai's names to indicate their spiritual revelation and new relationship with God. In its earliest Paleo form, the fifth letter was the sketch of a man with his hands raised as if to exclaim, "Hey…Look at that!"

Indeed, as day five develops, the sights are amazing. However, these sights often last only a split second as one or a group of the new beings of the air or water puts on a display. The less-than-productive, almost boring phase of day four is over. A new, dynamic phase is now in place. The sum or our preparation, work, and vision of our efforts in days one, two, three, and four now has a chance to yield some great progress. The advantage seems to go to the strong, those with the means to harvest these wily creatures. Meanwhile, the weak seem vulnerable to the flocks above and the schools below.

There is one factor of hope for the less strong or those of moderate means, and that is timing. If one can be ready at the right place at the right moment, great things can be accomplished, even with only modest means. Many a small team of warriors has ambushed a larger body of troops by this method. So also have small companies taken away market share from larger companies by bringing products or concepts to the market at agreeable moments. My point is that day five has the potential to change the status quo very quickly, and new players—those no one expected—will arrive and take their place on the stage, often at the expense of existing players.

If day four was a disappointment, day five will be a challenge. It can be very rewarding or it can be devastating. Consider our naturalist's situation as day four comes to a close. As darkness falls and day five begins, suddenly sounds of splashing in the water and shadows of movement in the sky will give the natural observer a sense that this indeed will be an interesting day. Excitement builds as once again there is new life.

It's not long before our naturalist discovers that this new life is very different from the vegetation of day three. These new creatures have mouths and teeth, the ability to communicate, and self-determination.

The vegetation of day three was easy to manage. Once you knew where a specific plant was, it did not move. The new life of day five, on the other hand, has some very different and disturbing characteristics. It will take some adjustment to be able to manage this new life form. Anyone who has fished or hunted wild game knows timing and location are the keys to success. Great amounts of time can be consumed fishing or hunting in the wrong place at the wrong time. It is also true that great catches can be made very quickly if you happen to be at the right place at the right time.

Some naturalists will be lucky and achieve great success without knowledge simply by being at the right place at the right time. The majority, however, will come up empty, and many will be bitten and even consumed.

The revealed use of the guiding lights of day four gives direction for when to rest and when to deploy our nets, when to be under cover and when to come out and play in this new world now dominated by the mobile biters.

It is better to be at the right place at the right time with little capability than to be at the wrong place at the wrong time, or caught in an ambush, with large capability. For many, during day five, luck appears to rule the day. Some seem just lucky to be at the right place at the right time. Others, seemingly well prepared, find themselves simply positioned badly, ending up empty handed, injured, or even consumed by some biter that no one saw coming.

On the other hand, the combination of a well-placed morsel of produce from day three and timing from day four offers the enlightened hunter or fisherman an opportunity for a successful ambush. Day five is quite a ride, and if you can find some success in day five, day six may be very good indeed.

One who knows the appointed times set by the lights of day four has an advantage. He knows when to rest and when to work. He also knows the food sources created on day three that the fish and birds must live on, so he has a sense of location as well.

It may not seem like a lot to work with, but these tools give you a chance for success. Without them you end up desolate, bitten, and exhausted! On top of that, the critters of day six have no intent of giving you a break. They are similar to those of day five, only these move about on dry land. Those doing well on day five will likely also do well on day six; however, those who struggled on day five may simply find that they have fewer places to hide.

Day five can only be mastered by properly using God's appointed times. To consistently prosper in this environment, learning to use the tools of day four is of great value. Leviticus 23 is a great starting point, and others will become clear as you meditate on God's appointed times.

The character of the sixth letter of the Hebrew alphabet is *vav*. In Paleo Hebrew the symbol is a tent peg, which has a meaning of "to secure or add to." Day six is the height of creation. Just as day four paralleled day one, and day five paralleled day two, so also day six parallels the new life of day three.

On day three, we had two distinct creation activities: the first appearance of dry land, and the appearance of new life in the form of vegetation. On day six, we also have two distinct creations: land animals, and the ultimate creation, humanity.

The first creation of day six only adds to the problems of day five—more mouths with teeth, more groups of creatures that can bite and overwhelm an unprepared individual. However, also in day six, the human makes his entrance into the story and is given dominion.

> God said: Let us make humankind, in our image according to our likeness! Let them have dominion over the fish of the sea, fowl of the heavens, animals, all earth, and all crawling things that crawl about upon the earth!
>
> —GENESIS 1:26,
> SCHOCKEN

Day six of the Creation story is simply full of complex new life. First there are animals in all varieties, suitable for various purposes, terrain, intake, and life cycles. Then, of course, humanity itself is created to take charge and rule over all that has been created.

Here is an interesting thought: Is it not unusual to have an ecosystem be created so complexly, and then bring in a ruler or overseer? Much has been made of the human being made in the image of God—but think of his lack of knowledge and understanding. He was, after all, created last, after all the other creations are put in place. Human had no part in the six days of Creation; now, with complete ignorance, he is put in charge.

Can this mean anything other than the idea that God wanted an ongoing, moment-by-moment, day-by-day relationship with His final created being? I think not!

For us who are finishing up a sixth of our own creation—be it a day, month, year, or a set of seven years—the lesson seems to be that all the pieces are in place. One can begin to understand fully what the divine light was trying to communicate. We see now the full connection to the *echad* unity of day one. In some ways, our work of these six days has yielded beyond our expectations, yet along the way we have suffered loss. Some of our dreams have developed beyond our wildest hopes, while others were lost amid the waves of days one and two, died for lack of new life in day four, or were bitten in day five or even day six.

The advent of day six and its transition from day five may be the most fluid transition of the whole set. The flying and swimming *nephesh chay* are now joined by the land walkers and runners. The hard and dangerous work of figuring out how to handle day five's creatures easily transfers to the management of the first created beings of day six.

It should be expected, however, that systems and relationships will become more complex. The creation of human in day six signals that a "God-like" being has entered the arena, and from now on his role will affect the rest of creation for good or evil.

The concurring sets of seven days, months, years, and sets of seven years, all running simultaneously, causes these reckonings to appear random. To the untrained eye, it seems that our world is not understandable or ordered. But a trained eye can see the clear purpose of each segment of time. In many respects, Creation is as much about the division of one element from another as it is about adding new elements. Early on, elements are moved from where they were before to new, defined, purposeful locations. For example, light is separated from darkness in day one. Water becomes restricted to its place above and below in day two; it is further restricted to the seas, lakes, and rivers, creating bare ground as the place for plants in day three.

Each new day brings new physical structures or beings into the world, but these new creations are set in their place apart from those that came before.

Fish are given the water, birds the air, and animals and human the land. All of these are separated into male and female form. Therefore, not only are these beings created, but they are properly set in their habitation, each with its unique role.

All of creation now awaits human's decision. Will he rest and worship the Creator? Or will he plunge ahead, trying to improve his enterprise, thereby worshipping the works of his hands?

Chapter 14
RETURN to the COVENANT

The Zenith Double,
a Time to Gather

THE DAY SEVEN TEMPTATION

God had finished, on the seventh day, his work that
he had made, and then he ceased, on the seventh day
from all his work that he had made.
—GENESIS 2:2,
SCHOCKEN

DAY SIX SEEMS very prosperous indeed. But day seven, a
day of rest, will have a profound effect on creation.

Signs of human's decision to abide by the instruction for
day seven are evident in day six. If he plans to rest and worship, he will be in preparation and gathering on day six. On
the other hand, if he plans to ignore the day of rest, he will
be working with the intent to build and grow his enterprise
in a linear fashion without regard for the revealed instruction. Sometimes he may get away with this lack of respect
for his Creator, but eventually there will be a day of reck-
oning, just as a modern automobile driver can only run so
many red lights before the odds catch up with him.

Think about the red lights of modern roadway inter-
sections. Are they helpful or harmful? Certainly, at times
when we have too much going on in our lives, they frustrate

us—but for the most part we accept them as necessary and good. So also are God's appointed times of rest. They are red lights along our highway of life, reminding us of Him and preventing us from being T-boned by the big trucks of life. Remember that all these new creatures of day six, just like the day five creatures, have *chay nephesh* (vigorous bodies with self-determination, and mouths and teeth for communication and biting). If we have figured out how to handle the creatures of day five, then the day six creatures can be managed in similar fashion with some adaptation. Day six should show great progress for the works of our hands. Day six should be full of good surprises.

The manna story of Exodus 16 gives us some instruction:

> Now on the sixth day they gathered twice as much bread, two omers for each one. When all the leaders of the congregation came and told Moses, then he said to them, "This is what the LORD meant: Tomorrow is a sabbath observance, a holy sabbath to the LORD. Bake what you will bake and boil what you will boil, and all that is left over put aside to be kept until morning." So they put it aside until morning, as Moses had ordered, and it did not become foul nor was there any worm in it. Moses said, "Eat it today, for today is a sabbath to the LORD; today you will not find it in the field. Six days you shall gather it, but on the seventh day, the sabbath, there will be none."
> —EXODUS 16:22–26

Day six, it turns out, is not just a day for great abundance, but is also a day of preparation for day seven, "the day of rest." There is instruction to gather double and prepare it. Here, then, is another counterintuitive moment. Having just seen everything improve so greatly, the call to prepare to cease building seems rather strange. After all the struggle, after all the loss, we now find ourselves with a fine, working system, and the instruction is to prepare to stop?

This is a moment for faith. Remember, we are not the Creator, only the created, made in the Creator's image. We need to learn how His creation works; tomorrow, day seven, will be our first day of intense training (or I should say, a "day of rest").

The fundamental lesson He wants all of us to learn is that rest is to be first in our lives. It is followed by six days of work, and the pattern continues in respect to months, years, and sets of seven years. Always remember man was created last on the sixth day, and he was put in charge of all of creation. His first day was a day of rest.

If we somehow find ourselves successful, or "made," in a sixth segment of time, we must know the purpose of God's direction for our next step. We must develop a place, ruled by the gracious timeline of "rest first," and then put forth our effort in the six days of work prepared ahead for us.

Can you hear an often-memorized portion of Ephesians 2 in the Genesis story?

> For by grace you have been saved through faith; and that not of yourselves, it is the gift of God; not as a result of works, so that no one may boast. For we are His workmanship, created in Christ Jesus for good works, which God prepared beforehand so that we would walk in them.
>
> —EPHESIANS 2:8–10

Grace and rest must be first in our lives; the works of our hands follow. And since our works are prepared ahead for us, it would also be wise to acknowledge our own cluelessness and great need for divine wisdom in our new role. Here is a moment not to be missed. Serious consideration needs to be given to harvest on day six.

Thinking of the sixth year as we look forward to the end of the seventh year and the release of debts, some things may need to be turned to liquid assets in order to meet the goal of complete balance. Look for things that seem more complex than necessary. These are the ones to move along. Clearly, day six should be the apex of accomplishment for this cycle of seven. The last book of the New Testament says the number of man is 666 and connects the three sixes with a very prideful individual, whom the writer calls the beast. It seems that while day six is the high point of the cycle, it is also a moment for a prideful man to make his biggest mistake.

Notice how the appointed times help us accomplish much in terms of stable gathering and blessing others with our work.

In contrast, consider the fate of the lucky naturalists—those who, by some set of happenstance, are at the right place at the right time and capture large quantities of this new life without understanding.

But as day six winds down, they are faced with a choice (whether they know it or not): will they be like the prideful beast, or will they be able to lay down their work and rest in day seven? In the end, it may be better for those who had meager years four, five, and six than for those who prospered without understanding.

The idea of stopping work just when things are going so well is a struggle for many people and organizations. Those in business, especially those with stockholders demanding return on their investments, are often inclined to produce resources twenty-four hours per day, seven days per week. The seventh day's instruction of rest seems to get in the way. Even those who know of its significance can't help but come up with some justification such as "good stewardship" or "serving needs of customers" as an excuse to blindly stay on the treadmill of ceaseless production.

Interestingly, even our own words tell us we should give the sevens another look. One of the most popular modern business proverbs goes like this: "Fail to plan, plan to fail." In these six words, we acknowledge that we must take time to plan. Why not do your planning on the day appointed for it?

Don't misunderstand; I am not talking about another workday where you do corporate strategic planning (although that's a good thing to do, and likely needs to be done shortly after the Sabbath). I am talking about a time of no responsibility, of letting your mind and body wander. Rest from normal activities and ponder the six days of work ahead of you. As you do, however, recognize that it is possible that a large amount of information may not be available to you at this moment in time.

The seventh letter of the Hebrew alphabet is *zayin*. Its original symbol was a mattock or a plow, a tool that made life easier. The meaning of the zayin is twofold: one of its definitions has to do with food, crops, and the fattening or feeding of animals; but it can also mean "weapon." The prophets wrote of beating swords into plowshares. It seems swords and plows are seventh-day symbols, telling us about two choices in this day, month, year, or set of seven years.

Since year seven is a year in which the instruction is to cease agricultural work by letting the land lie fallow, it is very likely a good year to make plows or improve your instruments of production for the years to come. However, if war is necessary, the production of plows may be turned to the production of swords and weapons, as the same tools are used to make each. So, in the seventh day or seventh year, what will it be? War or peace? A look at history reveals an uncanny connection to war and year seven, especially as year seven nears its end and a new cycle of seven years emerges.

It is while things may be humming along nicely when sudden shifts take place and a situation you thought was peaceful and prosperous becomes conflict, perhaps even war. This may very well take place in the seventh segment of time, but here is a key thought: in all likelihood, the changes will remain hidden until light comes on day one. As the Creation story says, "Let there be light."

Thus, we can see the importance of day seven as a time to prepare for the unexpected and observe our world with a keen eye. It is easy to understand why we would rest on the seventh. Even though we may not necessarily feel tired, the first days of the new seven may take all the energy we can give. It is better that we are ready.

As you recall, the element of time came into being on day four of Creation with the advent of the sun, moon, and stars. This division of time has some very unique characteristics. Its role in our lives is huge, yet without revelation it's as though there is nothing we can do with time except to march through it, one day after another. However, the information revealed by the biblical counts of seven shows additions, separations, and specific purposes for each segment of time. It also explains the reckonings that happen from time to time to those who choose to ignore the revealed appointments.

Human, as the last created being given the right to rule, has a decision to make. If he chooses to ignore the appointed times set by the Creator, then the divisions so neatly organized by the divine hand will begin to break down and the chaos of Genesis 1:2 will creep back into our ordered world. But there is an antidote for this creeping chaos: the gift of Sabbath that allows the return to divine order.

I started this discussion of seven segments of time with

an unusual approach. I chose to address the last segment, day seven, first. As I explained, my reason for this approach is because human was created last on the sixth day, and therefore he experiences day seven—Sabbath, a day of rest—as his first day.

The obvious implication for humanity is that day seven rest comes before the work of days one through six. So which is more important—work or rest?

There are six days set apart for work. However, for humanity, the day for rest is first, creating a rather interesting balance—a narrow path, if you will. Work is clearly important, as there are six days set apart for it; however, rest's day has the unique importance of being first. Again one cannot help but think of Jesus's words in Mark 2:27: "The Sabbath was made for man, and not man for the Sabbath."

Nonetheless, the answer to the question of which is more important has to be that both rest and work are important, but one cannot replace the other. For those who are unmotivated and inclined to sloth, the narrow walk of faith is clear: "work six." For those inclined to never rest, the narrow walk of faith is also clear: "rest first." In either rest or work, having the order correct and the elements of time in their proper place appears to be of great value.

This idea of Sabbath as a preparation for the six periods of work to come shows itself clearly for the household of faith in Deuteronomy 15 and 31. In these passages, Israel is instructed to release all debts on the seventh month of the seventh year to keep its economic system in a state of maximum flexibility. There are also instructions to release slaves and rest the agricultural land.

Each of these actions would also have the economic effect of new beginnings for the upcoming six years of work. They each demonstrate a willingness to lay down one's work, as well as a fervent belief in new birth, life from the dead, and hope beyond what our eyes can see.

For me, the adaptation of these concepts to modern life has a uniquely powerful draw. We could be so much more effective with our economic resources if we adapted these ideas to our lives. But how? How do we return to this system? What are the steps? Where do we start?

In chapter 12 I created a parallel for the first four biblical appointed times and festivals of Leviticus 23 with the first four days of Creation. I also pointed out that Exodus 23 calls for three annual pilgrimage festivals. The last of these is the seventh and final appointed time of Leviticus 23, the Feast of Tabernacles. During this festival in the seventh year of the biblical cycle, debts are forgiven.

The seventh month starts with a loud trumpet blast! It seems to say, "Hey! Wake up!" Rosh Hashanah is the fifth appointed time in the seventh-month cycle explained in Leviticus 23. It is a very appropriate event to be connected to the fifth day of Creation. The fifth appointed time is telling us when the seventh month starts. You need to be awake!

This wake-up call prepares us for the sixth appointed time: Yom Kippur, the Day of Atonement. The fact that the Day of Atonement is the sixth appointed time is quite telling. As we have seen, the sixth day is the day of highest achievement not only for our Creator, but also for us, the created. Therefore, a walk of faith calls for the most solemn day of the year for the sixth appointed time, Yom Kippur. And rightly so, for if our work has yielded greatly then this is the time to acknowledge our need of atonement. We must recognize our imperfection by surrendering our works. The traditional preparation for Yom Kippur is a review of all of one's relationships with his fellow man, and reparation if there is a need for amends. On Yom Kippur, atonement is made for the sins of the whole nation.

I find it remarkable that the fifth and sixth appointed times are designed to guide us to be the opposite of prideful. They do this first by instructing us to have the humility to make things right with our fellow man in the first nine days of month seven. Then, on the tenth of the month, the instruction is to afflict your soul. Traditionally, Yom Kippur is a day of fasting; a day of seeing our lack of perfection, our need of atonement.

What could be the meaning of this humbling of ourselves? What could be the purpose in the laying down of one's ego and pride during the sixth appointed time of Yom Kippur?

The answer is only available to those who understand and acknowledge the revelation. The answer is evident in the revealed seventh appointed time starting in the middle of the seventh month, on the fifteenth day, the full moon of the seventh month. This is the great joy of Sukkot, the Feast of Tabernacles.

What is so great about Sukkot? It is the great harvest festival. Many cultures around the world celebrate similarly, but the Hebrew version includes some very unique moments. At the end of six years, Sukkot marks the releasing of slaves, and at the end of the seventh year, the release of debts. Classical rabbis said that one has not known joy until one has been in Jerusalem during Sukkot; such was the reverence for the seventh appointed time of the biblical calendar. What could be more joyous and restful than being set free from the bondage of slavery or debt?

The seventh month is another picture of rest before work, and it shows us a couple different kinds of rest. Humility with others in repair of our human relationships is a type of rest. Humility before God, only possible after we have done all we can to repair our relationships with other humans, is another type of rest. And finally, celebrating a harvest and the release of slaves and debts also is a type of rest.

This expands our worldview about Sabbath. In Exodus, Moses informed Israel that Sabbath is a sign of the covenant:

> So the sons of Israel shall observe the sabbath, to celebrate the sabbath throughout their generations as a perpetual covenant. It is a sign between Me and the sons of Israel forever; for in six days the LORD made heaven and earth, but on the seventh day He ceased from labor, and was refreshed.
>
> —EXODUS 31:16–17

But which covenant? There are a number of covenants in the Bible, but one sticks out as a unique, "rest first" covenant. In Genesis 15, the covenant God makes with Abram is completed when a mysterious open flame and a glowing red furnace pass between cut-up pieces of animals. The passage records that Abram is asleep and in great darkness when this happens. In other words, he is at rest. His works will follow, but for the moment of receiving the covenant, he is at rest.

So also it appears that every time we rest in a set-apart seventh segment of time, we also are joining or rejoining Abram's "rest first" covenant. It could be said we "return to the covenant." After all, it was while he was at rest that Abram received a whole new direction and expectation for his life. I expect rest, as prescribed in the seventh segment of time, can and will open a new beginning for us as well.

In doing so, our sixth period of work will become more fulfilling and productive. Even more important, we will begin to have the means to fulfill another of God's promises to Abram: "In you all the families [nations] of the earth will be blessed" (Gen. 12:3).

A close study of Revelation 1 and 2 will reveal the identity of that mysterious open flame and glowing red furnace. But for now, this part of our study ends where it began: resting in day seven, at peace with our fellow man, released from slavery and debt, and anticipating guidance from the divine light of day one.

| 46 | 47 | 48 | 49 | 50 | 1 | 2 | 3 | 4 | 5 |

45									6
44									7
43									8
42									9
41									10
40									11

Part
THREE

39									12
38									13
37									14
36									15
35									16
34									17
33									18
32									19
31									20

| 30 | 29 | 28 | 27 | 26 | 25 | 24 | 23 | 22 | 21 |

Introduction to Part Three

GENESIS:
HOW WE ALL GOT HERE

I N THE BEGINNING, God created." English translations tell us this is how the Bible opens.

For the most part, we tend to think that the Creation part of the Bible is over by the middle of Genesis chapter 2. Once we encounter Adam naming the animals, for us the Creation story is over. Yet I would caution against that way of thinking. The whole book is called Genesis. To consider the Creation story to be concluded in chapter 2 is not wise, since all of the book is about beginnings. In fact, the Hebrew word *bê'rey'shit*, translated "Genesis," seems to carry a meaning of a preexisting beginning, or in other words a mysterious, unknowable beginning. So while it is true that the Creator has humankind—his highest form of Creation, made in His image—in place by the middle of chapter 2, the Creation story must continue not only through the whole Book of Genesis, but well past it. The Book of Genesis is only the beginning—and a preexisting beginning at that.

Anyone interested in origins would be wise to spend time thinking expansively about Genesis, keeping in mind that Genesis is only the beginning. What we find there continues on, in some form or another, to this day.

The psalmist repeatedly encouraged us to meditate on Moses's writings. He seemed to understand that patterns established in those early books continued into his day, and by extension, into our modern times as well.

Great institutions have been built for the study of the Bible. No book has been so dissected and discussed; yet do we even consider the notion that the events of Genesis, in pattern and type, are still happening? Are we looking for them to happen? Are we letting Genesis speak into our lives, or are we just thinking of it as history? Or worse yet, myth?

Here are some questions to think about:

- Does Adam and Eve's story still speak to our marriages?

- What about our relationships with our children? Does the story of Abraham and Isaac speak to that relationship?

- Our relationships with siblings?

- Our relationships with foreigners and strangers?

- Justice and judgment?

- Faith and righteousness?

- Repentance and new beginnings?

- Failure and renewal?

- Death and resurrection?

All these and more show up in Genesis, and it's only the beginning. The Book of Genesis appears to encompass twenty-five generations from Adam to Joseph's children. The writer seems to be implying that while the things described here are beginnings, they continue into the future. He is speaking to future generations, even to our day. He also seems to be implying that everything which happens in our day has its beginnings in Genesis. In other words, the trials, temptations, successes, and failures of the people we read about in Genesis continue, and we as humans created in God's image are still living out a Creation story of our own. It seems the world into which we have been placed is not a finished creation, but a place designed to be improved by us, the creative creation.

There are many areas of the Creation story that could be explored in great detail. For example, the light of day one is a mystery not only because where it comes from is undefined, but light itself is a mystery. What is light? How does it work? This is a question that could take up pages, but for this study, the element of time and its use in Genesis is our focus. Genesis seems to be telling us that our origins are greatly linked to certain elements of time and a specific family—Abraham's family. Regardless of what your tradition is or who history books say you are, each of us was mentioned in the very beginning of Abraham's story. Consider your role in Genesis 12:

> Now the LORD said to Abram, "Go forth from your country, and from your relatives and from your father's house, to the land which I will show you; and I will make you a great nation, and I will bless you, and make your name great; and so you shall be a blessing; and I will bless those who bless you, and the one who curses you I will curse. And in you all the families of the earth will be blessed."
>
> —GENESIS 12:1–3

While the writer of Genesis from this point on will focus on Abraham and his family's story, all peoples of the earth are to be affected by this one family. It will be in a positive way for those who bless, and a negative way for those who curse.

But how far will this family's effect go? Again, the writer shows us that this family will expand greatly:

> Now when Abram was ninety-nine years old, the LORD appeared to Abram and said to him, "I am God Almighty; walk before Me, and be blameless. I will establish My covenant between Me and you, and I will multiply you exceedingly." Abram fell on his face, and God talked with him, saying, "As for Me, behold, My covenant is with you, and you will be the father of a multitude of nations. No longer shall your name be called Abram, but your name shall be Abraham; for I have made you the father of a multitude of nations. I will make you exceedingly fruitful, and I will make nations of you, and kings will come forth from you."
>
> —GENESIS 17:1–6

This promise is repeated to Jacob, Abraham's grandson:

> Then God appeared to Jacob again when he came from Paddan-aram, and He blessed him. God said to him, "Your name is Jacob; you shall no longer be called Jacob, but Israel shall be your name." Thus He called him Israel. God also said to him, "I am God Almighty; be fruitful and multiply; a nation and a company of nations shall come from you, and kings shall come forth from you."
>
> —GENESIS 35:9–11

This becomes the family's destiny and legacy that is eventually spoken over Jacob's own grandsons, Joseph's sons:

> He blessed Joseph, and said, "The God before whom my fathers Abraham and Isaac walked, the God who has been my shepherd all my life to this day, the angel who has redeemed me from all evil, bless the lads; and may my name live on in them, and the names of my

fathers Abraham and Isaac; and may they grow into a multitude in the midst of the earth."

When Joseph saw that his father laid his right hand on Ephraim's head, it displeased him; and he grasped his father's hand to remove it from Ephraim's head to Manasseh's head. Joseph said to his father, "Not so, my father, for this one is the firstborn. Place your right hand on his head." But his father refused and said, "I know, my son, I know; he also will become a people and he also will be great. However, his younger brother shall be greater than he, and his descendants shall become a multitude of nations." He blessed them that day, saying, "By you Israel will pronounce blessing, saying, 'May God make you like Ephraim and Manasseh!'"

—GENESIS 48:15–20

Paul the New Testament writer is so steeped in this idea that his mention of it in Romans 4 is almost written as a "You know this, but I will say it anyway":

For the promise to Abraham or to his descendants that he would be heir of the world was not through the Law, but through the righteousness of faith.

—ROMANS 4:13

Paul is making an argument about faith and law. For him, the idea that Abraham's descendants will inherit the world is not a point of discussion. It is a fact from which he formulates his writings.

Therefore, the world that began in Genesis is not complete. It will be ultimately complete when Abraham and his descendants become heir of the world.

This has not happened yet. This is a work in progress. This is the Creation story continued. As Genesis closes,

Abraham's children are in Egypt, about to become slaves. A whole new beginning will be necessary.

And so it will be throughout the generations. Abraham's children will have ups and downs, often finding themselves in dire straits, in need of a new beginning. These new beginnings will appear in pattern and rhyme, very much like the original Creation story. Beginning with chaos, God will intervene step by step, adding and separating elements.

Abraham's children are called to be a blessing to all people. However, their ability to do so can only be realized if they learn how to synchronize their creative efforts with the Creator's original pattern.

Genesis indeed is the story of how humankind came to be, but even more important is the simple fact that Abraham's children have a destiny. The whole earth is waiting for a generation of Abraham's children to teach the masses how to harness the creative power of the universe. Some will bless and some will curse, but like Paul we know how the story ends. The ending is not even a point of discussion. The discussions revolve around how we who are created in God's image function to bring about His ultimate plan.

Isaiah tells us that the answers are from the beginning:

> Remember the former things long past, for I am God, and there is no other; I am God, and there is no one like Me, declaring the end from the beginning, and from ancient times things which have not been done, saying, "My purpose will be established, and I will accomplish all My good pleasure."
> —ISAIAH 46:9–10

The end it seems is told in Genesis; in other words, the patterns of Genesis will continue until a final conclusion of rest or heaven takes place—as Isaiah says, the end is declared from the beginning. As creators ourselves made in the image of the Creator, we have a role to play. But to succeed in our role, we need to bring the concepts found in Genesis into our day and give them opportunity. Otherwise, it will be left to another generation to clean up the mess we have made and make their own attempt at adapting the lessons "from the beginning" to their generation.

Chapter 15

JACOB'S DYSFUNCTIONAL HOUSEHOLD

JACOB IS A wonderful, counterintuitive character in the Book of Genesis. From his very beginning he was caught in a rivalry with his brother Esau. They wrestled even in their mother's womb.

> The children struggled together within her.
> —GENESIS 25:22

Esau, the firstborn, is strong—a man of the outdoors. Jacob is said to be at peace among the tents. What is the result of Jacob being among the tents? He has been listening and learning. Most timelines show that Jacob was about fifteen years old when his grandfather Abraham died, and we know teaching was one of the things for which Abraham was well known:

> Abraham will surely become a great and mighty nation, and in him all the nations of the earth will be blessed? For I have chosen him, so that he may command his children and his household after him to keep the way of the LORD by doing righteousness and justice, so that the LORD may bring upon Abraham what He has spoken about him.
> —GENESIS 18:18–19

I suspect Jacob was absorbing these lessons from Abraham while Esau was out in nature. Here is one of the first examples of the naturalist versus the revealed worldview. Esau is learning from what he sees in nature, while Jacob learns from his grandfather about the seven days of Creation, Noah's Flood, and Abraham's encounter with the light and the glowing furnace that passed between the pieces of cut-up animals.

As Jacob grows and matures, he realizes he has one problem. He is not firstborn, and therefore is not entitled to the birthright of his father. All this wonderful history and the covenant will be handed to his brother when his father, Isaac, dies. But Jacob notices that Esau really doesn't care about this ancient wisdom. Esau is excited about nature and has applied his mind to learning the ways of the animals so he can be a better hunter.

Jacob begins to look for an opportunity. Esau the hunter becomes the hunted. It was not happenstance that Jacob was cooking when Esau came in from a less-than-successful hunt. Jacob was likely working with the knowledge of time. Esau had expended great effort that day and had nothing to show for it.

As he had done to wild game many times while hunting, Esau was about to be ambushed—and food was the bait

Our modern understanding of how brothers should treat each other causes this story to generate almost universal sympathy for Esau. However, the writer of the Book of Hebrews takes a much different perspective:

> Pursue peace with all men, and the sanctification without which no one will see the Lord. See to it that no one comes short of the grace of God; that no root of bitterness springing up causes trouble, and by it many be defiled; that there be no immoral or godless

person like Esau, who sold his own birthright for a single meal. For you know that even afterwards, when he desired to inherit the blessing, he was rejected, for he found no place for repentance, though he sought for it with tears.

—HEBREWS 12:14–17

The Hebrews writer sees this story very differently than the many who have great sympathy for Esau. In fact, he turns Esau into the guilty party, and in doing so commends Jacob. What is Esau's sin? Very simply, indifference toward the birthright, giving it up for a single meal. By implication, Jacob, who cares greatly about the birthright, is applauded even though he clearly has not shown brotherly love. The story goes on to show Jacob, with his mother Rebekah's help, lying to steal Esau's blessing from his father as well.

There is little surprise when we learn Esau, the great hunter, wants to kill his brother Jacob, and we have no doubt that he has the skills to do so. Now Jacob is on the run, sent by his mother to her family's land to find safety and a wife. On his way he meets the God of his grandfather Abraham at Bethel—literally, "the house of God."

Things look pretty good when Jacob meets Rachel. Using some of his grandfather's training, Jacob offers seven years of work to secure her hand in marriage. This time, Jacob is the one ambushed by his father-in-law, Laban, who has two daughters and likes having Jacob work for him. Jacob will end up spending twenty years with Laban, time which was not full of extended family sweetness. Jacob put it this way when Laban confronts him, asking why he is leaving:

These twenty years I have been in your house; I served you fourteen years for your two daughters and six years for your flock, and you changed my wages ten times. If the God of my father, the God of Abraham,

and the fear of Isaac, had not been for me, surely now
you would have sent me away empty-handed.

—GENESIS 31:41–42

Clearly Jacob has had enough and wants to move on with
his life, yet he now has Laban's two daughters as wives. They
are in a contest with each other over Jacob's affection and who
can bear the most children. Interestingly, this contest brings
two more women into Jacob's family as surrogate wives, or
servant child bearers. By the time he is separated from Laban,
Jacob has twelve children: eleven sons and a daughter.

While Jacob leaves chaos behind by distancing himself
from Laban, he takes plenty of it with him in the form of
feuding sister-wives. He returns to the land of promise to
face his hunter brother, Esau.

By the time he wrestles the angel by the Jordan River and
is given the name Israel, he is certainly aware that he needs
divine help. He understands the time elements of seven, but
also understands that he needs the intervention of Abraham's God in order to live out the calling he has been given
by both the birthright and his father's blessing.

Esau is coming to meet Jacob with four hundred men,
and it seems obvious that Esau did not start out his journey
thinking peace. We expect that Jacob received divine intervention, causing his visits with his once angry brother to be
a peaceful meeting. Now Jacob brings his family into the
land promised, as two separate companies: Leah's clan first,
Rachel's second. Rachel is in possession of her father's idols,
which she stole.

Eventually these idols will be buried before the family
moves to Bethel, "the house of God." But it is key to note
that the beautiful Rachel and her offspring will always have
a predisposition for worship of other gods.

Jacob is back in the land at the place named the house of

God. Things are good, life is sweet, and God even gives him a new name, confirming for Jacob his father's and grandfather's covenant as his own:

> Then God appeared to Jacob again when he came from Paddan-aram, and He blessed him. God said to him, "Your name is Jacob; you shall no longer be called Jacob, but Israel shall be your name." Thus He called him Israel. God also said to him, "I am God Almighty; be fruitful and multiply; a nation and a company of nations shall come from you, and kings shall come forth from you. The land which I gave to Abraham and Isaac, I will give it to you, and I will give the land to your descendants after you."
> —GENESIS 35:9–12

For the moment, Jacob seems to have found rest and peace. After all he had been through, to be able to dwell at Bethel with confirmation of the covenant must have seemed like utopia to Jacob.

However, the division Laban's daughters had brought into his household was about to show itself again. Even though Jacob had become a godly man at peace with his brother and in covenant with God, another new beginning was happening. Chaos was brewing, and when it came to light, Jacob would lose much of his peace and joy.

Chapter 16

JOSEPH, the SPECIAL CHILD of YEAR SIX

A s a young man Joseph was handsome, smart, and favored by his father. However, the raw talent his father saw in him may not have been as evident to others as was his blatant arrogance. The depiction of Joseph in Genesis leaves little doubt that he was openly despised by his brothers.

Joseph was eleventh born of twelve brothers but the first-born of his mother, Rachel—Jacob's beautiful, beloved wife, the one for whom Jacob thought he was working seven years. Rachel's father deceives Jacob, who finds himself working fourteen years for Laban's two daughters and married to Leah, Rachel's sister, as well.

For the first years of marriage, Rachel was barren. Meanwhile Leah had six sons. In an attempt to better the situation, Rachel gave her servant girl to Jacob for procreation, and this produced two sons. Leah did likewise; Jacob has, in essence, four wives.

And then after a long wait, Rachel conceives and Joseph is born. With older siblings looking on, Jacob dotes on this beautiful son of his beloved wife. It is unlikely that the coat of many colors was the first time Jacob had favored Joseph. Add to this mix of family disharmony Joseph's dreams of leadership, and here develops the perfect storm of family discord.

The name Joseph means "to add." Joseph was born in the last years of the second seven-year cycle during which Jacob worked for Laban to pay for his wives. His name's connotation, "to add" or "increase," could well indicate that Joseph was born in a sixth year.

Just as the first chapter of Genesis speaks of seven days of Creation, cycles of seven years seem to have a role in the creation of Jacob's household. Exactly what understanding or knowledge was available to the pre-Mosaic Hebrews is certainly conjecture, but the idea that cycles of the earth are divided into sets of seven seems well established in the Creation story, and also in Jacob's family story.

It appears that Jacob has identified Joseph as the one who will carry on the birthright. In many respects, he makes the same decision his father, Isaac, made. Forgetting the pain of being the unloved son, Jacob chose to publicly prepare Joseph for taking over his role as the keeper of Abraham's covenant. As such, he also spent much time teaching Joseph all the things he had learned in the tents of his youth as he listened to his grandfather Abraham.

Jacob explains the roles of times and seasons to Joseph using his own life and the lives of his forbearers as an example of how God helps Abrahams's children: by repeatedly adding elements to their lives and giving them wisdom to separate these elements into functional segments, which can then, in time and with discipline, yield new life. Joseph is taught about the seventh day being man's first day, and that for man to be productive he needs to learn how to trust in God, and rest.

Joseph is taught that whatever elements come into his life must be put into separate, definable segments so they can be part of and have a role in future new life. Just as light needs to be separated from darkness, so also new elements entering our lives need to be put in compartments so they can be part of the process, but not overwhelm the work in progress.

For example, chaos ensues when Esau announces his

intent to kill Jacob. Jacob separates himself to Laban's house, and meets Rachel at the well. He desires to add her to his story, a very natural thing. Knowing the times, a skill he learned from his forbearers, he proposes to work seven years for her.

He is tricked and ends up with Rachel's sister Leah, but is also given Rachel seven days later; however, he must work for Laban an additional seven years. Again, an element is added to his story that seems to bring more chaos. But very soon, new life starts to happen. Leah is actually very fertile and brings forth four sons in very short order. Here again separation or division will need to take place to not allow chaos to overwhelm the progress. The clan will have two branches: Leah's branch and Rachel's branch. There is tension between them, but both yield life with Jacob's husbandry.

Once his fourteen years are complete, Jacob proposes to separate from Laban. But Laban wants him to stay, so a deal is struck to separate the wealth of flocks. This allows Jacob to earn a flock of his own, which he does very well, to the point of creating the jealousy of Laban and his sons.

Then Jacob makes a very interesting financial move. The timing is very clear. In the twentieth year that Jacob was with Laban, Jacob, sensing he is now despised, pulls up stakes and travels toward the Promised Land. In other words, in the sixth year of the third set of seven-year cycles counting from when he met Rachel, Jacob gathers his things and begins his pilgrimage.

Think carefully about what is happening here. How does this story fit into the Creation pattern?

Think of these twenty years in seven-year segments; they are seven-year segments four, five, and six years of segment six of the fifty-year Jubilee cycle.

In the Creation story, the sun, moon, and stars are created

on day four, but no new life occurs, just a setting of standards for the future. For Jacob, Rachel is his star. He works diligently for her. She was his guiding light. He is willing to bear these unproductive years because he knows it is the fourth set of seven years, a time of setting standards; he has vision for the life to come.

> Jacob served seven years for Rachel and they seemed to him but a few days because of his love for her.
> —GENESIS 29:20

Next comes the fifth set of seven years, as in day five of the Creation story, the wild and crazy life of birds and fish.

Could this not describe Jacob's household after he has married both of Laban's daughters? Life comes in abundance, but it is not a peaceful situation. Two camps exist, and they like to bite. Jacob, the man, made in the image of God, functioning as a creator, has his hands more than full, as he is now working with the new elements of women in his life. This creates a very lively clan with two distinct camps: Leah's and Rachel's. The pattern of teeming new life in two groups nipping at each other—surely Jacob's second set of seven years with Laban is in the pattern of day five.

In the sixth year of this fifth set of seven years, Joseph is born. As the story goes on, his birth year will become an anchor point on the timeline.

So when Jacob's fourteen years of working for his wives are over, the story is headed to a set of seven years that will have sixth-day characteristics. Jacob considers separating from Laban:

> Now it came about when Rachel had borne Joseph, that Jacob said to Laban, "Send me away, that I may go to my own place and to my own country. Give me my wives and my children for whom I have served you,

and let me depart; for you yourself know my service which I have rendered you." But Laban said to him, "If now it pleases you, stay with me; I have divined that the LORD has blessed me on your account."

—GENESIS 30:25–27

Laban, however, wants him to stay, so Jacob cuts a deal, separating the flock. Looking back at the Creation story, again we see that the animals were the first creation of day six. Jacob gathers his flock for most of six years. Then, understanding that man was made last on day six, Jacob looks over his possessions and decides that the sixth year of the sixth set of seven years is the time to gather all that is his, pull up stakes, and pilgrimage home in the sabbatical year.

He has his eye on the upcoming seven years as well, which will be a seventh set of seven years and should give him some rest, and in some respect create a completion to the matter. In his mind, being back on the land promised in the seventh set of seven years is a worthy goal and likely a place of refuge for the upcoming fifty-year Jubilee.

Jacob will have plenty of trials to face, but his relationship with Esau will be restored. God will meet with Jacob and give him a new name, reconfirming the promises made to Abraham and Isaac. Jacob will bring his family into the land in two separate groups. He will separate Rachel from her idols and bury the idols in Shechem. At least for a while things seem pretty good for the clan that is now named Israel.

But as a new fifty-year Jubilee cycle approaches, a new chaos is brewing. Jacob has not kept everything quite as separated as he should have. By showing public favoritism to Joseph, Jacob has caused a mixing that will produce extreme chaos. Joseph will have quite a challenge to have his story yield new life.

But Joseph has an advantage. The things he learned around the campfires of his youth will prove invaluable in Egypt.

See the chart of Jacob's and Joseph's calendar at 7and5orhymes.com.

Chapter 17
STORIES AROUND
the CAMPFIRE

THERE IS SOMETHING about an open fire and a night sky that releases the human heart in storytelling and reflection. Even in our modern world of electric lights and mobile devices, we still enjoy those summer nights around an open fire. If no one has anything to say, there is no awkwardness in simply listening to the crackling of the fire and smelling the smoke, leaning back once in a while to consider the Big Dipper or locate the North Star.

It's moments like this when even the most reserved among us may have something to say. A story is more easily told when one is looking into the fire and slowly choosing words. No idea, regardless of how silly it may have seemed in daylight, is beyond the realm of acceptance. Time ceases for a moment. Everyone loses themselves in their own thoughts, yet they are open to hearing others. The campfire is truly a unique human experience.

This phenomenon of the human spirit easily connects to the stories of Genesis. Abraham's covenant, as described in Genesis 15, contains the elements of stars and fire. For tent dwellers in a rather arid area of the world, I have to imagine evening fires were a valuable time for the older generation to pass along family traditions and history to the minds of the new generation through storytelling.

One event that predates the lives of Abraham, Isaac, and Jacob is the story of Noah and the Great Flood. Somehow, through thousands upon thousands of years, this tale of God's incredible power has been passed on to us with great precision when one considers it from a timing perspective:

> In the six hundredth year of Noah's life, in the second month, on the seventeenth day of the month, on the same day all the fountains of the great deep burst open, and the floodgates of the sky were opened. The rain fell upon the earth for forty days and forty nights.
>
> —GENESIS 7:11–12

Is it not astounding that this story that was likely transmitted orally for many generations has been preserved through the ages so perfectly that it even reveals the exact day of the beginning of the Flood? Not only do we know when the Flood started, but we can also pinpoint the occurrence of many other events along the way. Of course, forty days later, the rain stopped and the waters began to recede.

Consider the precise points of time described in these twelve verses:

> In the seventh month, on the seventeenth day of the month, the ark rested upon the mountains of Ararat. The water decreased steadily until the tenth month; in the tenth month, on the first day of the month, the tops of the mountains became visible.
>
> Then it came about at the end of forty days, that Noah opened the window of the ark which he had made; and he sent out a raven, and it flew here and there until the water was dried up from the earth. Then he sent out a dove from him, to see if the water was abated from the face of the land; but the dove found no resting place for the sole of her foot, so she returned to him into the ark, for the water was on the surface of all the earth. Then he put out his hand and took her, and brought her into the ark to himself. So

he waited yet another seven days; and again he sent out the dove from the ark. The dove came to him toward evening, and behold, in her beak was a freshly picked olive leaf. So Noah knew that the water was abated from the earth. Then he waited yet another seven days, and sent out the dove; but she did not return to him again.

Now it came about in the six hundred and first year, in the first month, on the first of the month, the water was dried up from the earth. Then Noah removed the covering of the ark, and looked, and behold, the surface of the ground was dried up. In the second month, on the twenty-seventh day of the month, the earth was dry. Then God spoke to Noah, saying, "Go out of the ark, you and your wife and your sons and your sons' wives with you."

—GENESIS 8:4–16

Why would the campfire storytellers be so careful to pass on the exact dates of all these events of Noah's Flood? Obviously today we have them in written form, and the danger of the dates being lost is minimal. But at this stage in history these were only oral stories. Why focus on the dates?

The reason is this: there is ancient wisdom hidden in these dates. First we are told the Flood occurred in "the six hundredth year of Noah's life." Looking back to the fifth chapter of Genesis, which marks the event of Noah's birth, the writer records his father Lamech's thoughts concerning the name of his new son:

Lamech lived one hundred and eighty-two years, and became the father of a son. Now he called his name Noah, saying, "This one will give us rest from our work and from the toil of our hands arising from the ground which the LORD has cursed."

—GENESIS 5:28–29

Due to the fact that Noah's name is associated with rest, and the Flood came in his six hundredth year (a number evenly divisible by the fifty-year Jubilee pattern), it therefore can be assumed that Noah's story is one of how good and evil are separated during the Jubilee year. After all, Jubilee is the biggest Sabbath, as it is the culmination of seven sets of seven years. Noah's story is a catastrophic wipeout of evil at the Jubilee.

Now we can understand why exact dates were passed along. Leviticus 25 and 26 record details of the seven-year Shmita and fifty-year Jubilee. At the end of the instructions, Moses adds these words, which sound an awful lot like the catastrophe of the great Flood, only without water:

> But if you do not obey Me and do not carry out all these commandments…you will sow your seed uselessly, for your enemies will eat it up. I will set My face against you so that you will be struck down before your enemies; and those who hate you will rule over you…I will also make your sky like iron and your earth like bronze. Your strength will be spent uselessly, for your land will not yield its produce and the trees of the land will not yield their fruit…I will make the land desolate so that your enemies who settle in it will be appalled over it. You, however, I will scatter among the nations and will draw out a sword after you, as your land becomes desolate and your cities become waste.
>
> Then the land will enjoy its sabbaths all the days of the desolation, while you are in your enemies' land; then the land will rest and enjoy its sabbaths. All the days of its desolation it will observe the rest which it did not observe on your sabbaths, while you were living on it…But you will perish among the nations, and your enemies' land will consume you.
>
> —LEVITICUS 26:14, 16–20, 32–34, 38

The placement of this dire warning immediately after instructions regarding the seven-and-fifty-year Sabbath is a critical statement: lack of observance of these yearlong Sabbaths triggers certain destruction.

The story of Noah's Flood contains dates that may help us understand the timing of when these destructions are carried out. Certainly, it appears that someone thought it would be important for future generations to know details about when to expect this separation of good and evil. Noah's story also tells us what renewal looks like, and when to expect signs that things will recover. Let's look at some of Noah's dates and see what they might be trying to tell us. To frame our story, we must first approach the passage describing the exit from the ark:

> Now it came about in the six hundred and first year, in the first month, on the first of the month, the water was dried up from the earth. Then Noah removed the covering of the ark, and looked, and behold, the surface of the ground was dried up. In the second month, on the twenty-seventh day of the month, the earth was dry. Then God spoke to Noah, saying, "Go out of the ark, you and your wife and your sons and your sons' wives with you."
> —GENESIS 8:13–16

The storyteller clearly wants us to know what year the story takes place because, again, only Noah and his family remain alive. He informs us that this new year is "the six hundred and first year" of Noah's life.

Apparently it was the first year of a new Jubilee cycle. Interestingly, even though the ground was dry on day one of the new year, Noah kept everyone on the ark for fifty-six or fifty-seven days, until the twenty-seventh day of the second month. Consider the counterintuitive message of this part of the story. Surely the ark smelled like a barn. There is some reason the teller of this story wants us to know that just because you see dry ground, it doesn't mean you can or should proceed. Finally, three days short of the third month, Noah and his family left the ark and offered sacrifices.

In short, the Flood began on the seventeenth day of the second month of the Jubilee year, seven days after Noah and his family moved into the ark. One year, one month, and ten days later—at the end of the second month of the first year of the Shmita and the Jubilee cycle—they left the ark to new life, offering sacrifices and worshipping. There seem to be implications that new life will begin in the third month of the new year, year one.

If this is the case, what else can we learn? What was the storyteller trying to make sure we did not miss by recounting all these dates in such detail?

First, notice that for everyone but Noah, the man with the revelation, the days leading up to the Flood seemed like all the days before. There were no signs in nature that gave others concern. Or perhaps they were blinded to the signs. After all, seeing animals loading into Noah's big wooden box should have at least made some stir. Yet only Noah and his family took refuge.

The days of the months in which these events occurred is interesting. The Flood starts on the seventeenth of the second month, but Noah and his family are in the ark seven days prior, on the tenth day of the month. Passover is held in the first month of the year; the tenth is the day for selecting the lamb sacrifice. The tenth day of the seventh month is also Yom Kippur, the Day of Atonement, when believers are called to fast and "afflict your souls."

Clearly, the spring and fall festivals have parallel patterns. There are divergent views as to whether the Flood began in the fall or the spring; however, the fact that it started in the second month reminds me that a person had the option to celebrate Passover in the second month if he was out of town or not fit to celebrate in the first month:

> Then the LORD spoke to Moses, saying, "Speak to the sons of Israel, saying, 'If any one of you or of your generations becomes unclean because of a dead person, or is on a distant journey, he may, however, observe the Passover to the LORD. In the second month on the fourteenth day at twilight, they shall observe it.'"
>
> —NUMBERS 9:9–11

This second-month Passover has one very interesting story recorded in 2 Chronicles 30. Hezekiah, who had only recently become king in Jerusalem, wished to celebrate Passover. But by the time the Levites cleaned up the temple from past disregard, the fourteenth day of the first month had passed. Hezekiah's Passover happened instead in the second month, as prescribed by Numbers 9. Hezekiah was the king of Judah, the southern and less wealthy of the two kingdoms, but he sent letters to all the tribes inviting them to his Passover. A study of history reveals that this was a last chance for many of those northern tribes to repent and turn back to God. Within a very short time after Hezekiah's belated Passover, many of those tribes disappeared, scattered to the four winds just as the prophets had warned.

The fact that the great Flood began in the second month may simply have been a gracious way of giving one last chance for repentance. Continuing with the Passover theme, the seventeenth, the day of the Flood is often associated with the Israelites crossing the Red Sea and Pharaoh's army being washed away—a very close parallel indeed. Personally, I tend to think the great Flood started in the second spring month.

I have put some thoughts on the middle segment of

Noah's story in Appendix Two. For now I want to focus on how Noah's time in the ark ends.

Noah and his family remain in the ark a year after the rain started. They have seen repeated signs that new life is just ahead for them, but they must wait in that stinky ark. Even on day one of the year when the ground is dry, they wait. They are only separated from that ark on the very last days of the second month.

As has been explained, the second day begins a time when space is made, but because of the scope of the catastrophe. Noah, hearing God, keeps his family on the ark until just before month three. He seems to be waiting until the last moment to enter this new situation due to the severity of the destruction. This story is, without a doubt, a story connected to the fifty-year Jubilee. It not only explains what to expect when devastation comes at the Jubilee but also gives us a window into how things look during recovery from an especially catastrophic destruction.

Keep in mind that although Noah was righteous, his life was immeasurably altered by the events of the Flood. We may discover that we can also survive a catastrophic fifty-year Jubilee or seven-year Shmita, but it is unlikely that we will be unaffected. Remember Noah's hesitation to come out of the ark even when the ground was dry. I expect there is wisdom in that wait—wisdom that is worth pondering.

I suspect it was around evening campfires that Jacob passed these stories to his favorite son. In time, Joseph would also dream about his role in the story.

Chapter 18

The DREAMER DISAPPEARS

Now Jacob lived in the land where his father had sojourned, in the land of Canaan. These are the records of the generations of Jacob.

Joseph, when seventeen years of age, was pasturing the flock with his brothers while he was still a youth, along with the sons of Bilhah and the sons of Zilpah, his father's wives. And Joseph brought back a bad report about them to their father. Now Israel loved Joseph more than all his sons, because he was the son of his old age; and he made him a varicolored tunic. His brothers saw that their father loved him more than all his brothers; and so they hated him and could not speak to him on friendly terms.

Then Joseph had a dream, and when he told it to his brothers, they hated him even more. He said to them, "Please listen to this dream which I have had; for behold, we were binding sheaves in the field, and lo, my sheaf rose up and also stood erect; and behold, your sheaves gathered around and bowed down to my sheaf." Then his brothers said to him, "Are you actually going to reign over us? Or are you really going to rule over us?" So they hated him even more for his dreams and for his words.

Now he had still another dream, and related it to his brothers, and said, "Lo, I have had still another dream; and behold, the sun and the moon and eleven stars were bowing down to me." He related it to his

father and to his brothers; and his father rebuked him
and said to him, "What is this dream that you have
had? Shall I and your mother and your brothers actually come to bow ourselves down before you to the
ground?" His brothers were jealous of him, but his
father kept the saying in mind.

—GENESIS 37:1–11

D ID JOSEPH RECEIVE a call from God? Absolutely! The
dreams showed him a glorious future, but they did not
show him the great cost it would take to get there. Interestingly, Joseph's dreams contain elements of the Creation
story. His first dream has a focus on plant life—but not just
any plant life: sustaining grains at harvest. Clearly this is a
day three reference. His second dream is of the sun, moon,
and stars, a clear reference to the fourth day of Creation.
These visions are not simply happenstance. They encompass
valuable predictive information about the future.

Of course, we know the story. Joseph was sold into
slavery in Egypt by his jealous brothers, and his father was
led to believe Joseph was dead. The arrogant Joseph disappears from our story. The next time we hear of him he is a
diligent slave in Potiphar's house, wise and discerning. We
are left to wonder what happened on the road to Egypt. The
arrogant boy has become a wise, God-fearing man; but that
does not mean he will have an easy path.

He is now seventeen years old, having been born in the
sixth year of the fifth set of seven years. We are likely just
past a fiftieth-year Jubilee, about to start a new Jubilee and
Shmita cycle very early in year one.

Since he knows Noah's story was about the events of a

Jubilee year, Joseph knows who was washed away this time: himself! But here he is, alive—in slavery, yes, but alive! Very much like Noah and his family, who had every resource they owned washed away in the Flood, so also Joseph, a slave, is stripped of every possession. Yet by the grace of God he is granted his life.

Joseph realizes that it was his own youthful arrogance that put him in this mess, but he knows that the future is yet to be written. He begins to seriously seek the God of Abraham, Isaac, and Jacob, and starts to live out the calling to be a blessing.

I find the story of Joseph's refusal of Potiphar's wife's sexual advances to be a very strong sign of his return to Abraham's covenant. As you will recall, God gave Abraham directions concerning the practice of circumcision. This mark on the male body is a sign of the covenant God made with Abraham. But it is not simply a sign with no purpose or logic. Through circumcision, God seems to speak loudly to any male, "What comes from there is important to me." In other words, God's promise to Abraham was land and children. Circumcision is a symbol reminding us that sexuality needs to be in a context conducive to the goals of the covenant. Potiphar's wife was not an option for Joseph if he was going to live out Abraham's covenant.

By showing restraint, Joseph was making a very strong statement that he hoped to one day have children of his own and to raise them as a wise and teaching father. Having intercourse with his master's wife would not further that goal. In all likelihood, it would lead to only trouble, even death.

Meanwhile, back at home, Joseph's father Jacob is devastated by the loss of his favorite son. His knowledge about time does not ease his pain. He recognizes that Joseph was lost at the end of the Jubilee. He has the evidence of the bloody coat obviously torn to pieces by the wild animal who carried his son's body off and consumed it.

For the Hebrew culture, this is an awful situation. Life is to be cherished. Death is understood as part of the natural course of things, but to die young, eaten by wild animals, is the worst of fates. Indeed, it is later a curse pronounced on Israel for disobedience to the covenant at Mount Sinai:

> Your carcasses will be food to all birds of the sky and to the beasts of the earth, and there will be no one to frighten them away.
> —DEUTERONOMY 28:26

For the Hebrew people, to die and be properly buried is one thing, but to be eaten by wild creatures is quite another. It means no one cared. Your life was insignificant and your death unnoticed.

Jacob is without hope concerning Joseph. His knowledge of time only confirms his hopelessness. I wonder if he noticed his other sons' lack of mourning for the death of their brother, or the new wealth they seem to have found.

Jacob must feel alone and vulnerable, yet he has Abraham's covenant, a promise of descendants and land. He had put all his effort into Joseph, but now he must rethink his part in Abraham's covenant.

By pronouncing that a wild beast had killed Joseph, Jacob may have been verbalizing his suspicions, indicating that his sons were more like the creatures of day six than men made in God's image. At this moment, Jacob's hope for the future must have taken a significant shift.

Even if he suspects that his sons had a role in Joseph's demise, it is they through whom Jacob will have to pass on Abraham's great calling. With Joseph gone, he must now set to work teaching the rest of his sons what it means to be the descendants of Abraham, Isaac, and Jacob.

In many respects, Jacob also understands that his own evil must be washed away, separated from him.

God has created a clean slate for all of them. The removal of Joseph from the house of his father opened up a new opportunity for the Creation story to play out in each of the brothers' lives.

Chapter 19

The FAITHFUL, INDUSTRIOUS JOSEPH

T HE YEARS MUST have passed slowly for Joseph, a young man full of energy with a dream and a calling, when he found himself wrongly imprisoned as a result of his wisdom and discipline. Sitting in that prison had to be heart-wrenching. I'm sure there were days he wanted to give up, but Joseph knew some things that gave him hope. He carried on his body the mark of circumcision, and he had demonstrated that he understood that it connected him to his great-grandfather Abraham and a covenant with God that promised a specific land and many descendants. For Joseph, the meaning was clear in his present circumstance: "Be careful what you do with this part of your body." In other words, even though he was a slave and far from his family, he was still hopeful for honorable fatherhood and manhood. He would not take a shortcut to sexual gratification.

This is the moment we know we are dealing with a new Joseph. In his father's house, Joseph was undisciplined in speech and deed. Whatever he wanted, he was given. Here was an opportunity to take the forbidden; by refusing Potiphar's wife he passed a great test. Unfortunately, he found himself in prison as a result.

Sitting in that cell, Joseph must have wondered what all of his troubles could mean. This new attitude of his caused him to do well even in prison, but surely he had time to think. One thing he considered was time. Joseph knew the seven-year count, and we can reconstruct his count by using some information the Bible gives us. Joseph seems to know that divisions are made at certain moments, as in the Creation story—light from darkness, waters above from waters below, dry ground from sea, in the same way the Hebrews believed that, at certain points, righteousness is separated from evil. Joseph seems to understand that all days are not alike, and that he was being prepared for a special moment.

When the cup bearer comes to him with a dream of three vines of grapes, Joseph recognizes the number three as a moment of truth, action, and the completion of a thing. He also recognizes vegetation as new life on the third day of the Creation story and that life is in the blood or the juice of the grape. Thus, he gives the cup bearer a favorable report. But when the baker comes with his dream of three baskets of bread being eaten by birds, Joseph immediately understands that this is a sign of death. The quantity of three will again indicate the moment of natural action, but the birds eating indicates the action is death. Thus, the cup bearer and the baker will be separated—one to renewed life, one to death.

As we have seen repeatedly, day three is connected with natural or logical events. It's supernatural, but in a very normal sort of way, just like a plant sprouting is supernatural and cannot completely be explained but can be replicated consistently.

Joseph's story tells us that the timing of his interpretation of the dreams for the cup bearer and the baker is important. In fact, the biblical language is very specific:

> Now it happened at the end of two full years that Pharaoh had a dream.
> —GENESIS 41:1

The text seems to indicate a period of exactly two years between the prisoners' dreams and Pharaoh's dream. Therefore, we are now at the beginning of the third year since Joseph had charged the cup bearer not to forget him. Here, once again, new life will begin on the third day.

The writer gives us another detail about the timing of this event in Joseph's story:

> Now Joseph was thirty years old when he stood before Pharaoh, king of Egypt.
>
> —GENESIS 41:46

We know he was seventeen when he was sold into slavery, and at the time of this event, he is thirty. We have deduced that he was born in year six of the fifth set of seven years. We suspect that he was sold into slavery in or very near the time of Jubilee, as Noah's Flood had taught him this is the time when evil is swept away. Now he stands in front of Pharaoh at the beginning of his third decade of life, knowing the third set of seven years since the Jubilee in which he was swept away from home is just about to begin.

Joseph knew what time it was. He now clearly understood that the fifty-year Jubilee had been in effect when he was seventeen and separated from his family thirteen years earlier. As he stood before Pharaoh, Joseph knew this was the end of the second set of seven years and a third set of seven years was just ahead. He expected new life in the third set of seven years. He knew he had a calling, and with the help of his God he had done all he could to live righteously since the day he found himself a slave.

He was also counting the separations in his life. He had been separated from his family, from Potiphar's house, and he expected his dreams and calling might very well come to pass if he could be separated from this prison.

Therefore, when he heard Pharaoh's dream, Joseph knew

exactly what it meant. He knew this was his moment. He had revelation knowledge about time. Pharaoh and his men only had an understanding of the observable natural rhythms. Joseph had revealed knowledge of seven and three as it relates to time—specifically, God's appointed times.

See the chart of Jacob's and Joseph's calendar at 7and5orhymes.com.

Chapter 20

JOSEPH KNEW the TIME

T HE WRITER OF Psalm 81 gives us some insight into Joseph's process for recovering his life with these words:

> Sing for joy to God our strength; shout joyfully to the God of Jacob. Raise a song, strike the timbrel, the sweet sounding lyre with the harp. Blow the trumpet at the new moon, at the full moon, on our feast day. For it is a statute for Israel, an ordinance of the God of Jacob. He established it for a testimony in Joseph when he went throughout the land of Egypt. I heard a language that I did not know: "I relieved his shoulder of the burden."
>
> —PSALM 81:1–6

In this passage, we learn something about Joseph's adventure that is not recorded in Genesis. We learn that the moon and its marking of time was a key element in relieving Joseph from his burden of slavery and imprisonment.

The psalmist specifically mentions the new moon. A new moon also had a role in saving David's life in 1 Samuel 20. For Joseph, the new moon has similar significance.

The only new moon listed among the appointed times of Leviticus 23 is the new moon of the seventh month. Yet as you read through the rest of the Hebrew Bible, you often run across the new moon mentioned in the same sentence as the weekly Sabbath.

For example:

> Then Solomon offered burnt offerings to the LORD on the
> altar of the LORD which he had built before the porch;
> and did so according to the daily rule, offering them up
> according to the commandment of Moses, for the sabbaths,
> the new moons and the three annual feasts—the Feast of
> Unleavened Bread, the Feast of Weeks and the Feast of
> Booths. —2 CHRONICLES 8:12–13

Here, as in many other passages, a new moon is listed along with Sabbath and other appointed times. What was its role? For the ancient Hebrews, the new moon was a time for revelation, set apart for seeking God and finding direction for the month ahead.

As with any spiritual act, the new moon can also be observed with malicious intentions or a wicked heart. The Book of Hosea indicates that new moons can cause considerable harm for those who have abandoned God's ways:

> They have dealt treacherously against the LORD, for
> they have borne illegitimate children. Now the new
> moon will devour them with their land.
> —HOSEA 5:7

Isaiah, prophesying in the same time frame, sees the same problem for all of the appointed times, and very quickly gets to the heart of the issue:

> Bring your worthless offerings no longer, incense is
> an abomination to Me. New moon and sabbath, the
> calling of assemblies—I cannot endure iniquity and
> the solemn assembly. I hate your new moon festi-
> vals and your appointed feasts, they have become a
> burden to Me; I am weary of bearing them. So when
> you spread out your hands in prayer, I will hide My

eyes from you; yes, even though you multiply prayers,
I will not listen. Your hands are covered with blood.
—ISAIAH 1:13–15

The purpose of the moedim (the appointed times) is that
we can be the blessing to which Abraham is called. When
we stop being that blessing, it is likely that the new moons
and other appointed times become damaging to us rather
than helpful.

Consider Joseph again. He finds himself in slavery shortly
after he tells his two dreams to his family. Each of these
dreams contains an element of the Creation days: the plant
life of day three; and the sun, moon, and stars of day four.
Joseph's father expressed what everyone understood:

> He related it to his father and to his brothers; and his
> father rebuked him and said to him, "What is this
> dream that you have had? Shall I and your mother and
> your brothers actually come to bow ourselves down
> before you to the ground?"
> —GENESIS 37:10

Jacob doubts that Joseph actually had a dream, and
seems to imply that Joseph made it up. But there is no mystery about what the dreams mean. Clearly, for Jacob these
dreams are about a time in the future. However, to make
the accusation that Joseph simply fabricated these ideas
means that in their culture, plant life and the sun, moon,
and stars are clear references to elements in time. This is
specifically apparent in the case of the sun, moon, and stars.
They are the marks of day four, and day four is all about setting appointed times.

Joseph, the one who dreams of big things, is almost immediately removed from the family. He finds himself in slavery,
and his father thinks he is dead. Whatever knowledge

Joseph had was not enough to overcome his lack of brotherly love. In spite of his dreams (or maybe because of them), he was swept away at the beginning of a new Jubilee cycle, just as the evildoers of Noah's story. But he remains alive. Now, just like Isaiah instructs the people of his day, Joseph changes and purposes to become the blessing Abraham's children are called to be:

> "Wash yourselves, make yourselves clean; remove the evil of your deeds from My sight. Cease to do evil, learn to do good; seek justice, reprove the ruthless, defend the orphan, plead for the widow. Come now, and let us reason together," says the LORD, "Though your sins are as scarlet, they will be as white as snow; though they are red like crimson, they will be like wool. "If you consent and obey, You will eat the best of the land; "But if you refuse and rebel, You will be devoured by the sword." Truly, the mouth of the LORD has spoken.
>
> —ISAIAH 1:16–20

In this passage Isaiah is explaining that, just as Joseph discovered, as long as someone is alive, they have the opportunity to repent and change. The appointed times can either be a great ally or a formidable opponent. However, mere knowledge of them is not enough. In fact, using them arrogantly or with impure intentions is a recipe for disaster.

In Egypt, Joseph sets his heart toward becoming faithful to his great-grandfather's calling: being a blessing to all nations. He knows what time it is, but more importantly, he is now committed to his family's calling.

That commitment, along with the knowledge of the moedim, would set him free and save many lives, including those of the family members who had dispatched him to Egypt years earlier.

As he stands in front of Pharaoh, Joseph knows this is his moment. He is thirty years old, and the time is right. It is around the time of the new moon at the beginning of year one in the third set of seven years. Joseph knows that this is the time of new life, the third set of seven years. He also knows that the fourth set of seven years will not bring new life, only the setting of standards and guiding lights.

When Pharaoh tells of his dreams, Joseph knows exactly what they mean.

Seven fat cows followed by seven lean cows.

Seven fat ears of grain followed by seven lean ears of grain.

Pharaoh's dreams are a miracle, but Joseph's interpretation comes from understanding. Joseph knows the time and explains the meaning of the dreams based on this knowledge. The storyteller is passing on some ancient wisdom.

Of course, our story is far from over. The seven plentiful years occur just as Joseph predicted, but when the fourth set of seven years begins, there is famine in Egypt. Just as we discussed in Part Two, day three is rich and full of new life, while day four is weak and poor, but sets new standards.

Joseph's interpretation allows Egypt to be well prepared for the famine, and therefore spares many lives.

The story swings back to Joseph's family in northern Canaan. They are not faring well in the fourth set of seven years. They are out of food, and Jacob has heard that there is food in Egypt.

He dispatches ten of his sons to go to Egypt and collect grain. The timing of this first trip is not clear, but it seems logical that it is near the end of year one of the fourth set of seven years. This is a time when the chaos that has overtaken the house of Jacob will "come to light." Joseph, still working within his understanding of time, is not about to reveal himself at this juncture. Instead, he is going to work with the times as he understands them to test and even purify his brothers.

He accuses his brothers of being spies, interrogates them, and puts them in jail for three days before finally releasing nine of them. He withholds Simeon, and tells his brothers not to come back unless they bring their youngest brother, Benjamin, as proof of their relation. Joseph knows this is a tall order since Benjamin is the youngest son of his father's favorite wife. He sends his estranged brothers on their way with food. In order to scare them even more, he puts their money in their bags of grain so when they open their sacks they will worry about being accused of stealing.

Back with their families, food quickly runs out, and Jacob wants his sons to go back to Egypt for more. They refuse to do so unless Benjamin goes along. Jacob is very unhappy with this arrangement, but eventually yields to it after Judah gives his personal pledge to protect Benjamin. Upon arriving in Egypt, Joseph treats them well, even providing a feast for them. He is again using his knowledge in order to build up his reputation as a diviner. He purposefully places each brother at the feast by their order of birth, causing no small stir among the brothers.

Joseph is still not ready to reveal who he is; he has a further test. Again, he fills their sacks and sends them off, and again he puts their money back in their sacks. But in Benjamin's sack he puts his silver goblet.

The next morning the brothers set out, but they do not get very far before Joseph sends his head servant to overtake them and accuse them of stealing his silver goblet. Of course, it's found in Benjamin's sack, causing great distress for all the brothers. None is more fearful than Judah, who gave his personal pledge to return Benjamin to his father. Joseph insists on taking Benjamin as his slave, sending the rest home in sadness and guilt.

This is the moment of truth. Joseph wants to know if his brothers will protect a son of Rachel. Judah steps forward and offers himself in place of Benjamin, explaining that to go home without Benjamin would grieve his father to the point of death.

Joseph can hide his identity no longer, and finally reveals that he is their brother. The narrator gives us an important date. Joseph explains to his brothers that two years of famine are already past, but five years of famine remain. Therefore, he wants them to bring the whole family to him in Egypt.

This means that Joseph's brothers are bowing before him in the fourth set of seven years at the beginning of the third year. Consider again Joseph's dreams from when he was seventeen.

In the first dream, sheaves of grain bow down (i.e., plant life of day three). Likewise, in the second dream it is the sun, moon, and stars bowing down (i.e., the lights of day four).

Based on our timing sequence, the brothers finally bow to Joseph at the beginning of the third year of the fourth set of seven years. Could it possibly be a mere coincidence that Joseph's two dreams have the symbolism of third-day plant life and fourth-day sun, moon, and stars in them? When you think about it, his dreams' symbolism of days three and four fit in two ways. They project not only exactly when his family will bow to him, but also which two sets of seven will be the time of his rise to power.

Surely the storyteller is trying to pass along knowledge about dates and times. Otherwise he would not have given us the specific details of time. The story of Joseph is profound, with plenty of lessons for life and examples of right living and wrong living. To this day this story is well known throughout the world, but the time element it describes is rarely explored.

The next time element the writer gives us is that of Jacob living in Egypt seventeen years before his death. On our timeline, that would put Jacob's final blessing and death in the sixth year of the sixth seven-year cycle. This is a seemingly fitting moment for an introduction to the twelve tribes of Israel and the unique gifting of each tribe. Jacob's vision of the future has some surprises that affect us to this day.

See the chart of Jacob's and Joseph's calendar at 7and5orhymes.com.

Chapter 21

JACOB'S BLESSING

WITH THE ARRIVAL of the whole clan in Egypt, the realization sets in that the descendants of Israel are saved by being in a foreign land. Jacob has time to think about his hopes for Joseph and now his hope for his whole clan. Back when Joseph was a youth, Jacob was so taken by the boy that he hardly noticed his other children. His thinking was that Joseph was the child of promise just like his father, Isaac, had been, and just like he wanted to be (even though he had to use deceitful means).

The promise that God gave Abraham and Isaac mattered greatly to Jacob. Over the years that he thought Joseph was dead, Jacob had looked carefully at the skills and attributes of each of his sons. Believing Joseph to be dead, he recognized that he had clearly been wrong about Joseph being the one to carry forward the covenant. Jacob had sought God about how the covenant was to be passed to the next generation. He had come to grips with the idea that maybe he had twelve sons for a reason; maybe they were all of value for God's purposes in future generations. He knew them all well by now. He had seen them pull together in the difficult famine and look out for each other, even protecting Benjamin, the only son left of his beloved Rachel. They even seemed to respect his love of Rachel now.

With Joseph back in his life, Jacob now realizes the sixth-year birth was a telltale sign about Joseph and his greatness. But Jacob sees in Joseph an Egyptian. He knows he must somehow keep the clans of Israel living as Hebrews. If they become Egyptians, the revealed knowledge will slip away, and within a few generations Abraham's covenant will be lost among the pyramids.

Yet there is no denying Joseph's skill and gifting; therefore, Jacob makes a plan. He knows he is near the end of life and must implement what God has shown him. Calling Joseph in with his two sons, Jacob adopts Joseph's two sons as his own, in essence giving Joseph a double portion, or the birthright, just as Joseph's name means "to add."

Jacob makes it a point to set the younger son, Ephraim, ahead of Joseph's older son, Manasseh, in a prophetic foretelling of which tribe of Joseph will be predominate. This the third time in the Genesis story where the second-born child is given preference. Isaac was set ahead of Ishmael, Jacob ahead of Esau, and now Ephraim is set ahead of Manasseh. The implications of this are worth pondering. Could it be that second-born sons are more empathetic leaders? Is there a message here?

At this point one may think that Jacob has put the clan in the hands of Joseph the Egyptian. But Jacob is not done. Now he calls in all twelve sons and he blesses each one. Genesis describes it this way:

> All these are the twelve tribes of Israel, and this is what their father said to them when he blessed them. He blessed them, every one with the blessing appropriate to him.
>
> —GENESIS 49:28

The most significant surprise is the blessing on Judah. Jacob says:

> Judah, your brothers shall praise you; your hand shall be on the neck of your enemies; your father's sons

shall bow down to you. Judah is a lion's whelp; from
the prey, my son, you have gone up. He couches, he
lies down as a lion, and as a lion, who dares rouse him
up? The scepter shall not depart from Judah, nor the
ruler's staff from between his feet, until Shiloh comes,
and to him shall be the obedience of the peoples.

—GENESIS 49:8–10

Jacob makes Judah the leader, not Joseph. Joseph is clearly
blessed with large offspring and wealth, but to Judah belongs
"the scepter" and "the obedience of the peoples."

Jacob has passed leadership to Leah's son, their fourth
born. Judah has shown leadership and he is clearly Hebrew,
not Egyptian. Jacob has recognized that in order to be a
powerful entity, these brothers must work together. He
knows their diverse talents and recognizes that when they
work together they can accomplish great things. Just like
day four of Creation sets the standard of time, so now the
fourth son sets the standard of leadership. In both cases no
one saw it coming. In the Creation story no one expects the
sun, moon, and stars to show up on day four, setting standards of time after new life has already sprouted; so also
everyone thought leadership was Joseph's, since he had
brought about the new life they were now experiencing.

Joseph was the logical, natural choice, but Jacob had revelation. The leader was Judah.

This choice is in some senses quite problematic. But Jacob
has lived with family quarrels all his life. He is not interested in a false peace. The peace the brothers know now in
Egypt will disappear as this generation dies off. Jacob recognizes that leadership for Judah's descendants, put in in tension with wealth and a large census for Joseph's descendants,
will either force working together or division. Divided they
will be weak; together they will be strong, Jacob set things
up so they will have to be united as brothers to be strong.

The Book of 1 Chronicles gives us a comprehensive paragraph about how Jacob's blessing was understood in the later generations:

> Now the sons of Reuben the firstborn of Israel (for he was the firstborn, but because he defiled his father's bed, his birthright was given to the sons of Joseph the son of Israel; so that he is not enrolled in the genealogy according to the birthright. Though Judah prevailed over his brothers, and from him came the leader, yet the birthright belonged to Joseph).
>
> —1 CHRONICLES 5:1–2

It was understood that Joseph received the birthright and with it a double portion of this earth's blessings. But Jacob had taken the role of leader, usually given to the receiver of the birthright, and given it to Judah, and so it was understood generations later as the Chronicler is preparing to tell us about David's kingdom. David, the last-born son of Jesse from the tribe of Judah. David, almost forgotten while out tending the sheep when Samuel came to town to anoint the new king. He will become the gold standard of leaders, and every prophet will write of dreams of one of his sons coming forward to lead again.

Joseph's wealthy multitudes will always be tempted to break away from Judah's leadership. Judah's leadership will always be tempted to tyranny. Joseph's clans are always capable of leaving because they have the wealth and the large populations. But whenever Joseph's clans attempt to appoint their own leaders, they very soon find themselves involved in pagan ways of idol worship, as patterned by Joseph's mother, Rachel, when she carried her father's idols into the Promised Land.

The Book of Genesis is just that—a book of beginnings. Taken as a whole it has patterns that exist to this day. These patterns run through many areas of life and touch on many themes: creativity and time, man and woman, temptation and failure. And in its later chapters, Genesis deals with brotherhood, and Jacob's realization that each of his sons has value and is needed for the clan to prosper. Specifically his blessing on the two especially gifted sons, Joseph and Judah, opens a line of thought that speaks to us to this day.

Jacob has set up a nonlinear leadership model that seemingly has worked only twice in history. The first time it worked was when Joshua and Caleb led the tribes into the land. These two spies who gave a good report—Joshua from the tribe of Ephraim (Joseph's younger son) and Caleb from the tribe of Judah—set the example for the generation who took the land forty years after they left Egypt. The second time this model worked was when David, from the tribe of Judah, was able to gather all twelve tribes under his leadership and usher in Israel's finest era.

It is interesting to note that Joseph's tribes held the Jezreel Valley and its key access points. This piece of ground is not only very fertile but also holds the key trade route from Egypt to points east and north. Clearly the land Joseph's tribes possessed in David's time were the region of the largest population and wealth. It is interesting that they were willing to follow a young man who got his start as a shepherd on the marginal soils of Judah.

David and then Solomon were able to hold this powerful united kingdom together for about seventy years, and then it all fell apart under Solomon's son Rehoboam.

The kings of Judah never recovered those northern wealthy tribes. The sons of Joseph appointed kings of their own, from the tribe of Ephraim. Just as Jacob's blessing had anticipated, Joseph's younger son had preeminence. The modern archaeological record shows they were wealthy, and the biblical record shows that they very quickly were paganized by the nations who traveled their trade routes, and justice, mercy, and faith quickly became of little value. The prophets Amos and Hosea walked these fertile northern trade routes calling for repentance, to no avail. The nation began to break down about eighty years after Solomon's death, as towns were lost to invaders. Israelites were taken as prisoners and slaves, while others began to flee.

By 722 BC (about two hundred years after Solomon) Samaria, the seat of the northern kingdom, is overrun by Assyria. Shortly after Hezekiah's Passover, Joseph's tribes, with their large numbers and great wealth, disappear from view, having been thoroughly scattered to all corners of the globe, where they remain to this day.

As far as modern Israel is concerned, to both the Jewish state and the Jewish religion, Joseph is considered dead.

Yet among the nations a line of Abraham's children wait for the moment when God will quicken them to the morality they know deep in their being. They will awaken to the knowledge of the revealed counts of seven and fifty, and once again they will have a role in building a kingdom greater than Solomon's. Of course they will need leadership from the brother they walked away from. Every Christian should have some vision of who it is that will lead this rebuilding of David's kingdom.

So I end Part Three with this question: Does the seven-and-fifty-year economic cycle intrigue you? If it does, then perhaps Joseph is alive among the nations.

CONCLUSION

WE LIVE IN a world where human interaction is very unstable. Economic and political systems are in a constant state of flux. Despite the best efforts of the United Nations, wars continue to pop up in a variety of locales all over the globe. Despite the best efforts of the International Money Fund and the developed world's central bankers, economic turmoil and market collapses continue to surprise even the most modern (and supposedly enlightened) nations of the world.

Because of the contemporary certainty that man is most important, it never occurs to most moderns that the answer to finding stability is to do less. This natural human arrogance leads mankind to the certainty that he can on his own fix dysfunction, perceived or real. Natural man's instincts are to jump in and immediately work on finding an answer to all difficulties.

The Creation story suggests another way. It suggests man take a lower opinion of himself—that he find a way to acknowledge his Creator in all his successes. This mind-set advocates that man take a time of rest and become reflective concerning his role in creation before he attempts to place order on the dysfunction or chaos he finds in his world.

As we have seen, there is a rhythm built into our world; therefore, finding the appropriate time to rest, and even how to rest, requires instruction. Thankfully, that instruction is in the world's best-selling book, the Bible.

The instruction is that "rest is first" for humans, followed by six days of work, which sets a pattern that allows us to create in the same rhythm as the Creator. In addition, we are made aware of the distinct features of each of the seven days of Creation. This understanding, then—along with knowing what day, week, month, year, or set of seven years it is—gives us the ability to make good decisions about how to focus our efforts.

These instructions about time have us working when others are fearfully saying, "It is no use to try!" They also lead us to rest and generosity when others greedily reach for gain.

Therefore, what remains is for humankind to learn and implement the revealed instruction. This can only happen when the instructions of God reside with the Spirit of God within a man or a woman.

Those who pursue the instructions of God without the Spirit of God will become entangled with rules and lawyerly work-arounds. On the other hand, those who pursue the Spirit of God without the instructions of God will often find themselves on a path lacking sound direction, and can even find themselves involved with things that are destructive.

Our Creator has set things up so that we, the created in His image, also become part of and active in the creation, following the patterns of beginnings as described in the Book of Genesis. It is also clearly true that as we, the created in His image, begin to implement these concepts in our lives, we become an active part in the creation process by adding new elements to our story and placing each new element into its appropriate role.

The new or renewed covenant spoken of in Jeremiah 31 and Ezekiel 36 is very clear: the Spirit of God will write the instructions of God on the hearts of His people. As has been shown in this study, each of us has a role in pursuing these things.

May we all do our part, and may those days come quickly.

Appendix 1

HOPE for THOSE in IMPOSSIBLE SITUATIONS

SOMEONE IS GOING to read this book and realize that they are in a situation where it is impossible to enter into the patterns laid out in this book for many years, maybe even many decades. Regardless of why you find yourself in that situation, I want to offer you hope. One verse that has had a great resurgence in recent years gives me pause every time I hear it—not only because of its message, which is wonderful, but because of its historical setting:

> "For I know the plans that I have for you," declares the LORD, "plans for welfare and not for calamity to give you a future and a hope."
> —JEREMIAH 29:11

I seriously doubt that most modern believers who quote this verse understand that Jeremiah is speaking to a people who have been put on a forced march by a foreign army away from their burning city, homes, and all that they knew.

These people had just experienced horrid, unmentionable things. Many lost children, loved ones, and their own dignity. They are being sent to a land hundreds of miles away, where their language is not spoken, their God is not worshipped, and their way of life is not followed.

You, dear reader, may also find yourself in an impossible situation. And if your heart now longs to live inside God's appointed times but your circumstances will not allow it, you are not the first, nor are you alone. Listen to these words from the prophet Zephaniah:

> "I will gather those who grieve about the appointed times—they came from you, O Zion; the reproach of exile is a burden on them. Behold, I am going to deal at that time with all your oppressors, I will save the lame and gather the outcast, and I will turn their shame into praise and renown in all the earth. At that time I will bring you in, even at the time when I gather you together; indeed, I will give you renown and praise among all the peoples of the earth, when I restore your fortunes before your eyes," says the LORD.
>
> —ZEPHANIAH 3:18–20

Notice the promise is to those who mourn or grieve the appointed times, the moedim. It is a promise to gather, a promise to deal with your oppressors, a promise to remove the shame and turn it into praise, and a promise to restore your fortunes.

Our Father has appointed times, and He wants to meet us at those times, even if we are in the most difficult of circumstances. He still wants you to mark the day, the week, the new moon, and the year He has set apart, and to let Him know your heart and your request.

Appendix 2

MORE THOUGHTS
on NOAH'S STORY

THE RAIN AND fountains of the deep continued to pour out water for forty turns of the earth. Then, on the twenty-seventh day of the third month (assuming a thirty-day lunar cycle), the rain stopped. One can imagine the heavens were very bright with clear skies. By now we know what day three, month three, or year three means. The ceasing of the rain told Noah and his family that they were going to live. Then, at the end of month three, near the beginning of month four, a new standard of life was being set. You can be sure that the light of the sun, moon, and stars during that fourth month were brighter than ever before, a clear sign of a new beginning for Noah and his family. Yet the ark is afloat with no ground in sight.

Finally, "in the seventh month, on the seventeenth day of the month, the ark rested upon the mountains of Ararat" (Gen. 8:4). There it is again: the seventeenth. On the first seventeenth, the evil was washed away by the floodwaters. On the seventeenth of the seventh month, the ark lands safely. The ark found its place of rest in the seventh month on day three of week three. This date is also the third day of what Leviticus 23 tells us is the Feast of Tabernacles, the annual, joyful harvest celebration. Profound!

The story continues, "In the tenth month, on the first day of the month, the tops of the mountains became visible" (Gen. 8:5).

The tenth. Imagine that. A completed seven months. Add three months and it seems the tenth month confirms a new life for Noah, giving him a sight of bare ground (even if it is only mountaintops in the distance). Keep in mind our discussion in chapter eight of the two sets of seven months in the annual cycle. Recall that month seven of the fall is also month one of the winter set of seven months. If this is so, then the first day of the tenth month is actually the moment of transition from month three to month four. This scenario also sets up the next details about time.

Our storyteller takes an interesting turn:

> Then it came about at the end of forty days, that Noah opened the window of the ark which he had made; and he sent out a raven, and it flew here and there until the water was dried up from the earth. Then he sent out a dove from him, to see if the water was abated from the face of the land; but the dove found no resting place for the sole of her foot, so she returned to him into the ark, for the water was on the surface of all the earth. Then he put out his hand and took her, and brought her into the ark to himself. So he waited yet another seven days; and again he sent out the dove from the ark. The dove came to him toward evening, and behold, in her beak was a freshly picked olive leaf. So Noah knew that the water was abated from the earth. Then he waited yet another seven days, and sent out the dove; but she did not return to him again.
> —GENESIS 8:6–12

Noah has birds on the ark and decides to put them to use. This information alone should have you thinking of day five, as birds are day five creatures.

Therefore, if the tenth month (in which the tops of the mountains were seen) was the end of month three and the beginning of month four, then this part of the story says that forty days later Noah sent out a scavenger bird: the raven.

A count from the first day of the tenth month will put us at the tenth day of the eleventh month, or the tenth day in the fifth month of the winter cycle. (I know this is difficult to grasp. Reread it until you understand, or go back to chapter 8 and read the section about month seven, the month of Tishrei.)

There are four events of releasing birds from the ark every seven days. The last dove to be released, the one that does not return, goes out in the first week of month six and finds new life.

Noah's story seems to tell us how day five works during a recovery. Early on, there is only food for scavengers. But as each set of seven days passes, things get incrementally better. Eventually, as day five transitions to day six, even birds of peace who only feed on new life have no need of greater protection or food.

The story of the birds should be understood as the fifth day leading into a sixth day. Therefore, month five began with the earth sustaining only scavengers, but ends with a dove finding a home just as we enter month six. One more sign that things are on the mend.

Yet Noah and his family stay on the stinky boat for a few more months, waiting for their time to inherit the earth.

Noah's story is most fascinating because of its details and its connection via images to the Creation story. In essence Noah's story is a re-Creation story, and if we can hear it, the details teach us about re-creations in our own lives.

Appendix 3

The FATHER'S APPOINTED TIMES ARE DESIGNED to PUT US in the RIGHT ATTITUDE, at the PROPER PLACE, at the PROPER TIME

IT IS OBVIOUS the seven-day week is made up of two sets of three days and a Sabbath. Rhyme clearly exists between day one and day four, day two and day five, as well as day three and day six. For the believer, it is also plain to see that the revealed instruction strongly connects day one to day seven, unifying all seven days into a single entity or unit.

The appointed time of day four, as explained by Leviticus 23, put the first three appointed times (moedim) in month one and the last three in month seven. This leaves only the fourth festival to be celebrated in any other month. As it turns out, the fourth moedim, Shavuot/Pentecost, is celebrated early in month three, connected to the third appointed time, "First Fruits," by a fifty-day count.

So what is going on here? A number of teachers have been using the method of chiastic breakdown to find the central message of certain biblical texts. Hollisa Alewine has done so with the Creation story, opening up the possibility that the day four creation of the sun, moon, and stars has a connection to the Father's appointed times, the central point of the biblical sevens. Hollisa Alewine's work can be found at www.thecreationgospel.com.

I have come to believe there is a common and normal creation pattern that the writer explains to us in Genesis 1. At many points along the way, as we live through this pattern, it is counterintuitive. For example, we are seeing no sign of new life in day one, day two, or even into the morning of day three, yet these are considered work days. One needs to have some understanding of the revealed in order to have the hope necessary to put forth effort in what appears to be a lifeless, hopeless situation. In retrospect, the new life of day three makes sense; but during the early days, only the knowledge of the revelation gives us hope.

On the other end of the seven days, the idea that we are to rest on day seven, just after the strong productivity of day six, is also very counterintuitive, going against all our natural inclinations.

The creation pattern of Genesis 1 is indeed one experienced by all mankind, even if one is ignorant of it or chooses to ignore it.

But the celestial lights of day four, in conjunction with the revelation that these lights are for the setting of times and seasons, change things for believers who embrace the instruction. While the natural observer will be tripped up again and again by the creation pattern, the believer is shown a different way. Not only is he aware of the events of each day and their transitions, but he is given instruction for his actions at the most critical junctures. It is obvious the most critical juncture falls on day seven as it transitions to day one. The second critical juncture is when day three transitions to day four.

Let's look at these two moments in time by examining the calendar of appointed times in Leviticus 23. This instruction is likely attempting to teach us how to engage creation and to successfully become creators in the Creator's image.

As has been our practice, we will look at month seven first. The fifth appointed time of Leviticus 23 is the Feast of Trumpets, which falls on the first day of the seventh month. This day is a call to attention, only ten days before the sixth appointed time, the Day of Atonement/Yom Kippur. The trumpet blasts on day one of this month seven call each person to prepare for the most sacred day of the year. Believers are commanded to humble themselves, make things right with their fellow man, and in contemplation, prepare their hearts for the atonement made on their behalf, a result of their imperfections.

I find it very instructive that Yom Kippur is the sixth appointed time of the annual calendar, in complete contrast to the natural pride man experiences in his day six. Yom Kippur is purposefully a day of contrition for the believer:

> Also the tenth day of this seventh month shall be the Day of Atonement. It shall be a holy convocation for you; you shall afflict your souls, and offer an offering made by fire to the LORD.
> —LEVITICUS 23:27, NKJV

The instructions to "humble yourself" or "afflict your souls" are generally expressed as a fast. Consider that day six of Creation is the high point, the zenith of all Creation. Consider that we, as mankind created in the Creator's image, likely also had our greatest creation in month six. As believers, we have gathered in a harvest of plenty. The fact that Yom Kippur is the sixth appointed time seems to instruct the believer to acknowledge this time of great humility. In all likelihood, month six was the moment of greatest accomplishment, and therefore, also the greatest temptation for pride in one's accomplishments or creation.

Yet, here at the sixth appointed time (moedim), the instruction is to afflict your soul, consider your imperfection, humble yourself before your fellow man, and recognize your need of an atoning sacrifice in order to restore you to proper relationship with your Creator. This again is a counterintuitive instruction. Rather than gather together in the great harvest of month six and throw a big party in month seven, the instruction for the first ten days of month seven is to humble yourself and seek God with all your heart, soul, and being, to be restored to completeness.

Why? Because there is nothing sweeter than celebrating in unity with others and feeling God's blessing on the celebration.

So what about the harvest party?

> On exactly the fifteenth day of the seventh month, when you have gathered in the crops of the land, you shall celebrate the feast of the LORD for seven days, with a rest on the first day and a rest on the eighth day. Now on the first day you shall take for yourselves the foliage of beautiful trees, palm branches and boughs of leafy trees and willows of the brook, and you shall rejoice before the LORD your God for seven days. You shall thus celebrate it as a feast to the LORD for seven days in the year. It shall be a perpetual statute throughout your generations; you shall celebrate it in the seventh month. You shall live in booths for seven days; all the native-born in Israel shall live in booths, so that your generations may know that I had the sons of Israel live in booths when I brought them out from the land of Egypt. I am the LORD your God.
> —LEVITICUS 23:39–43

The seventh appointed time begins on the fifteenth day, the very beginning of week three, at the full moon. This eight-day event is the greatest celebration of the biblical calendar. In year seven, it is the time when all debts are released. It is quite appropriate that it takes place in week three of month seven, showing us a combination of new, bare ground from which life must spring forth on day three and rest on day seven.

This is even more significant when you add the specific instruction for the Feast of Tabernacles in the seventh year:

> Then Moses commanded them, saying, "At the end of every seven years, at the time of the year of remission of debts, at the Feast of Booths, when all Israel comes to appear before the LORD your God at the place which He will choose, you shall read this law in front of all Israel in their hearing. Assemble the people, the men and the women and children and the alien who is in your town, so that they may hear and learn and fear the LORD your God, and be careful to observe all the words of this law."
>
> —DEUTERONOMY 31:10–12

Notice also that the instructions for living as a free society, the Torah, is to be reread to everyone at this time in year seven. Interesting that the remission of debts and the verbal repetition of the instructions for life are connected. This seems to mark a new start and designate the path to walk.

Traditionally, these eight days in the waning summer are the most joyous event of the year. It was said by the classical rabbis that one has not experienced joy until he or she has been in Jerusalem for Sukkot, the Feast of Tabernacles.

In the seventh month of the fiftieth year, the land is returned to the families who originally owned it:

> You are also to count off seven sabbaths of years for yourself, seven times seven years, so that you have

the time of the seven sabbaths of years, namely, forty-nine years. You shall then sound a ram's horn abroad on the tenth day of the seventh month; on the day of atonement you shall sound a horn all through your land. You shall thus consecrate the fiftieth year and proclaim a release through the land to all its inhabitants. It shall be a jubilee for you, and each of you shall return to his own property, and each of you shall return to his family.

—LEVITICUS 25:8–10

Interestingly, the return of the land to the original families is at Yom Kippur. Why return land on the Day of Atonement? It seems there is a connection to these verses from Leviticus:

The land, moreover, shall not be sold permanently, for the land is Mine; for you are but aliens and sojourners with Me. Thus for every piece of your property, you are to provide for the redemption of the land.

—LEVITICUS 25:23–24

Since the land is God's, it is returned to the original family on the day set aside to restore God's people to a proper relationship with Him. The text makes it clear that we are "but aliens and sojourners" with God; thus the land cannot be permanently sold.

The events of month seven teach us more about what a Sabbath should be: a time of contemplation of our imperfections, and an attempt to restore our relationships with our fellow man and our Creator. Then there is a joyful harvest celebration, setting people free of debts in year seven, and returning land to original families in year fifty.

These events of month seven prepare us for the annual winter months. As I have pointed out, in the case of the annual calendar, winter is the beginning of the year. It parallels the instruction from Genesis 1 that states the days of Creation begin at sundown, thus night is the beginning of a new day. As night is associated with sleep or rest, so also is winter, the dormant growth season. God is consistent in His instruction that rest is first for man. Therefore, it will be six or seven months of winter before we reach month one of the summer season of annual appointed times.

The biblical calendar is very logical and unswerving in its emphasis of rest. It teaches us that the beginning of the seventh month, the end of summer, is the start of a new year, the beginning of the annual calendar.

As we discussed in chapter 8, this could be very confusing for many who are new to the biblical calendar, especially considering the below instruction in Exodus:

> Now the LORD said to Moses and Aaron in the land of Egypt, "This month shall be the beginning of months for you; it is to be the first month of the year to you. Speak to all the congregation of Israel, saying, 'On the tenth of this month they are each one to take a lamb for themselves, according to their fathers' households, a lamb for each household. Now if the household is too small for a lamb, then he and his neighbor nearest to his house are to take one according to the number of persons in them; according to what each man should eat, you are to divide the lamb. Your lamb shall be an unblemished male a year old; you may take it from the sheep or from the goats.'"
>
> —EXODUS 12:1–5

Clearly this passage is talking about the spring month of Passover in verse two where Moses writes, "This month shall be the beginning of months for you; it is to be the first month of the year to you." At this point our Western, logical mind-set simply assumes this must be the demarcation from one year to the next. But if that were the case, it would break the "rest first" pattern. What Moses is communicating is that this is the beginning of your agricultural or life-giving year. The annual year began six or seven months earlier. But now that the winter rest is over, the winter barley is about to yield its first grain and everyone is anxious to get into the fields.

So what are the instructions? Exodus tells us the instructions to the Israelite slaves in the days just before they were released from Egypt. As we will see, it would have taken some discipline to implement these instructions.

"On the tenth day of the month bring a lamb into the house" (see Exodus 12:3). It's spring, it's time for cleaning. Why are they bringing an animal into the house? Of all things, a jumpy, playful yearling lamb or goat. The young children are delighted. They scratch its ears and wrestle with their new pet. Everyone examines this young creature and sees clearly its fine qualities and innocent perfection.

The slaying of that lamb on the evening of the fourth day, the fourteenth, at twilight cannot help but draw tears from all in the house. Yet it is that lamb's blood on the doorpost and lintel that signals the death angel to pass over the house in his awful harvest of the firstborn that night.

The call now comes to hurry and leave the slavery of the Egyptians, taking with them the Egyptians' silver and gold. They are not allowing their slaves to go but encouraging them to go, giving them their treasures to encourage them to leave quickly. This will not be a casual, pleasant journey. Even the bread will be flat due to the haste of departure. It will be known through the ages as the bread of freedom.

But this quick separation is critical, for in only few days Pharaoh will change his mind and send his troops out in an attempt to enslave God's people once again.

Leviticus 23 gives us these instructions for remembering this amazing month one of the new life part of the year:

> "These are the appointed times of the LORD, holy convocations which you shall proclaim at the times appointed for them. In the first month, on the fourteenth day of the month at twilight is the LORD's Passover. Then on the fifteenth day of the same month there is the Feast of Unleavened Bread to the LORD; for seven days you shall eat unleavened bread. On the first day you shall have a holy convocation; you shall not do any laborious work. But for seven days you shall present an offering by fire to the LORD. On the seventh day is a holy convocation; you shall not do any laborious work."
>
> Then the LORD spoke to Moses, saying, "Speak to the sons of Israel and say to them, 'When you enter the land which I am going to give to you and reap its harvest, then you shall bring in the sheaf of the first fruits of your harvest to the priest. He shall wave the sheaf before the LORD for you to be accepted; on the day after the sabbath the priest shall wave it. Now on the day when you wave the sheaf, you shall offer a male lamb one year old without defect for a burnt offering to the LORD. Its grain offering shall then be two-tenths of an ephah of fine flour mixed with oil, an offering by fire to the LORD for a soothing aroma, with its drink offering, a fourth of a hin of wine. Until this same day, until you have brought in the offering of your God, you shall eat neither bread nor roasted grain nor new growth. It is to be a perpetual statute throughout your generations in all your dwelling places.'"
>
> —LEVITICUS 23:4–14

There are three specific appointments in this month one. The first is Passover, which begins at twilight on the fourteenth, the time the lamb was killed and its blood put on the doorposts and lintel. Think about this moedim's connection to day one of Creation. Think about the the turmoil and commotion around the killing of that lamb—the children crying, the sadness of heart in every adult—and then the sudden revelation and joy when it is realized that the very children who cried last night are alive today because of the properly applied bloody cross on the doorway.

The divine light of understanding that dawned for the Israelites in that morning of the fifteenth day of the month—day one of week three in month one—when all the Egyptians mourned the loss of their firstborn, had to be a tremendous "light of day one" revelation. Now everyone understood the evil of slavery, both Israelite and Egyptian. By keeping the appointed time and its instructions, the Israelites had escaped unharmed. The Egyptians found themselves in revealed chaos, as they now understood their guilt. The Israelites plundered the Egyptians, asking for and receiving silver and gold, which was given to them out of panic. This is the first of the seven moedim clearly showing divine light on the chaos of evil slavery. The appointed time separated slave from master just as light was separated from darkness on day one.

The second appointment lasts for the whole week, starting on the fifteenth. The instruction is to eat unleavened bread as a reminder to separate from evil quickly. In time, yeast would be compared to sin:

> Your boasting is not good. Do you not know that a little leaven leavens the whole lump of dough? Clean out the old leaven so that you may be a new lump, just as you are in fact unleavened. For Christ our Passover also has been sacrificed. Therefore let us celebrate the feast, not with old leaven, nor with the leaven of

> malice and wickedness, but with the unleavened bread
> of sincerity and truth.
>
> —1 CORINTHIANS 5:6–8

Here the very Jewish apostle Paul encourages us to remember to flee sin as we celebrate the events of week three of month one.

A week of unleavened bread seems to have a relationship with day two of Creation, when space for life was created by the separation of the waters into two sections, water above and water below. This also seems to be the meaning of the second moedim. Eating only unleavened bread seems to remind us that only separation from sin, slavery, and evil of all kinds can prepare us for the new life to come. Therefore, there is a clear connection between the second appointed time and day two of Creation.

The third appointed time is First Fruits. The instructions are, "When you enter the land which I am going to give to you and reap its harvest, then you shall bring in the sheaf of the first fruits of your harvest to the priest. He shall wave the sheaf before the LORD for you to be accepted; on the day after the sabbath the priest shall wave it" (Lev. 23:10–11).

Many arguments are made over which day this is to be celebrated. This appointed time does not have a specified day of the month associated with it, only the instruction to celebrate it "the day after the Sabbath." Some feel the text speaks of the weekly Sabbath; some feel it speaks of the day after the fifteenth, which is a Sabbath according to verses 6 and 7:

> Then on the fifteenth day of the same month there is
> the Feast of Unleavened Bread to the LORD; for seven
> days you shall eat unleavened bread. On the first day
> you shall have a holy convocation; you shall not do any
> laborious work.
>
> —LEVITICUS 23:6–7

I chose not to get into this argument, but only to point out that this third appointed time of First Fruits clearly has a connection to day three of Creation.

The waving of the first harvest of barley is clearly connected to the advent of plant life bearing fruit and seed on day three of the Creation story. Even more significant are the day-three connections to the story of those escaped slaves stuck at the Red Sea with the Egyptians closing in on them, having changed their minds about letting go of their slaves (not to mention their gold and silver).

Here again is a profound moment. Having survived the death angel and left Egypt quickly as free people, flat bread in hand, the Israelites are now in need of a third miracle. Indeed, this miracle occurs in perfect parallel to day three of Creation, when land is separated from water and new life springs forth. So also these Israelites, with evil behind them and closing in fast, are rewarded for their faith by a new separation of water and a revelation of dry land as a path to new life.

Notice the miracle was dry ground separated from waters of chaos on either side. Notice also that new life was achieved by walking to the other bank of the sea. A very natural, logical act! Once that bare ground appeared, no one could have stopped the Israelites from walking that path to new life and freedom, just as no one can stop plant life from emerging from the ground if it has all the elements of the first three days of Creation: water, light, space or air, and bare ground.

Here we also learn something new about day three. The Egyptians, of course, try to follow in a last-ditch effort to retrieve their wealth of slaves, gold, and silver. As a result, on this day three, they are washed away with finality, and the Israelites celebrate a threefold salvation. Isaiah has an interesting take on these events:

Was it not You who dried up the sea, the waters of the
great deep; who made the depths of the sea a pathway
for the redeemed to cross over?

—ISAIAH 51:10

For Isaiah, the Israelites were already redeemed as they
stood pinned between the Egyptians and the Red Sea. The
blood of a lamb had saved their firstborn; and their wise,
quick separation from evil put them in a perfect position
for the final act that would separate them from the evil of
slavery forever.

Maybe the reason we are not sure about the exact timing
of the third appointed time of First Fruits is because that's
how it is in life. We are redeemed by the blood of the Lamb
and are reminded to be separated from sin and evil by an
annual unleavened bread experience, but our final separation from evil still awaits us. A day three of new life is yet to
be seen in its fullness. Wow, what a pattern!

This is also how things work in life. As creators, we need
to sacrifice in order to acquire enlightenment as a day one
activity. We need to separate ourselves from evil things that
bind us as a day two activity. These two things must happen
before we can expect a day three path to open before us.

Here is where the believer needs to find a balance. Obviously, days one, two, and three are work days, but among
these days is clear, divine guidance in the form of light, separation of chaos, and creation of dry paths amidst the chaos.
While we have our hands at work, we are also seeking guidance appropriate for each day.

The appointed times of month seven and month one have
uniquely prepared us for the summer growth season. By now
we have rested properly in month seven, and repaired our
relationships with our fellow man and God. Now in month
one we have received divine light as guidance, separated

from evil, and walked a dry path that has destroyed our enemies.

This is what you call being ahead of the curve (lingo describing the horizontal, right hand side of the bell curve). It is still only the first month, and we have incorporated moedim five, six, and seven safely in our Sabbath experience. Moedim one, two, and three are already behind us by the end of Passover season in the third week of month one. Challenges remain, but as we finish up month one, we really are in an extremely strong aleph, ox-like position (an ox head is the Paleo symbol for the first letter of the Hebrew alphabet).

There is one more appointed time on our calendar:

> You shall also count for yourselves from the day after the sabbath, from the day when you brought in the sheaf of the wave offering; there shall be seven complete sabbaths. You shall count fifty days to the day after the seventh sabbath; then you shall present a new grain offering to the LORD. You shall bring in from your dwelling places two loaves of bread for a wave offering, made of two-tenths of an ephah; they shall be of a fine flour, baked with leaven as first fruits to the LORD.
>
> —LEVITICUS 23:15–17

The fourth appointed time is Shavuot, Pentecost. As I mentioned earlier, a chiastic breakdown of the seven days of Creation puts day four as the centerpiece or focus of the whole set. Here I am, dealing with it last, but in all likelihood, it is the central message of the revealed instruction. We will see why in a moment.

Again, we have the same phrase "the day after the Sabbath" for a counting of seven weeks or fifty days, bringing us to this moedim unsure of its exact day in the lunar cycle.

But any count of fifty days from week three of the first month will bring us to the early part of month three. Here is the believer's amazing situation having rested through moedim five, six, and seven in month seven, and having followed the instructions for moedim one, two, and three in month one. In each case, clear connection to the appropriate day of the Creation story was evident. Now we come to a most interesting juncture.

The fourth moedim falls early in month three. This information alone tells us that we are looking at the setting of standards—day four.

Divine light has shown into our situation, separation of chaos has created space, and the bare ground has appeared for the springing forth of new life—day three.

This is exactly what happens at Shavuot/Pentecost. This appointed time is a celebration of the giving of the Torah to Moses at Mount Sinai. Moses explained the purpose of this instruction perfectly:

> See, I have set before you today life and prosperity, and death and adversity; in that I command you today to love the LORD your God, to walk in His ways and to keep His commandments and His statutes and His judgments, that you may live and multiply, and that the LORD your God may bless you in the land where you are entering to possess it. But if your heart turns away and you will not obey, but are drawn away and worship other gods and serve them, I declare to you today that you shall surely perish. You will not prolong your days in the land where you are crossing the Jordan to enter and possess it. I call heaven and earth to witness against you today, that I have set before you life and death, the blessing and the curse. So choose life in order that you may live, you and your descendants, by loving the LORD your God, by obeying His voice,

and by holding fast to Him; for this is your life and
the length of your days, that you may live in the land
which the LORD swore to your fathers, to Abraham,
Isaac, and Jacob, to give them.

—DEUTERONOMY 30:15–20

The giving of the Torah early in month three set the standard for achieving new life for this large ragtag community of former slaves. These instructions are written in the
imperative. At times they seem harsh, but their purpose is
clear: to create a nation of free people who can interact with
each other and with their Creator in a mutually beneficial
capacity. All these instructions are designed to strengthen
the common man and pull down any leader who would seek
to oppress this community of God's free people.

Alas, even these words, which were meant to set people
free, were either ignored or misused to allow binding and
enslavement of a different kind. This occurred in the centuries that followed the giving of the Torah on Mount Sinai,
when the descendants of those who saw the fire on the
mountain stopped applying these instructions to their lives.
They soon fell into the ways of the nations around them.
Forgetting the meaning of Sabbath and the other appointed
times, they became caught up in constant nature-worship
of the sun, moon, and stars. Abandoning the new life of day
three and the moedim of day four, they became a people
without knowledge of the God of their ancestors, completely
lost to the nation of Israel.

Meanwhile, another group held fast to the writings of
Moses. Throughout the centuries they have been able to
keep their status as Israel, and to continue to pass on to
their children God's instructions and appointed times.
However, along the way their application of the law has at
times become the very bondage it was intended to throw

off. This occurs in the rigid application of minute details and man-made additions to the Torah called "hedges around the law." At times this resulted in a misplaced focus directed away from the weighty matters of the Torah—justice, mercy, and faith.

This second group is to be respected and appreciated. It is the Jewish people who have held on to and passed down all of these ancient writings that form the basis for living as a community of free people. No other documents can claim to deliver such freedom.

This leads to the second historical event that happened on this date early in month three:

> When the day of Pentecost had come, they were all together in one place. And suddenly there came from heaven a noise like a violent rushing wind, and it filled the whole house where they were sitting. And there appeared to them tongues as of fire distributing themselves, and they rested on each one of them. And they were all filled with the Holy Spirit and began to speak with other tongues, as the Spirit was giving them utterance.
>
> —ACTS 2:1–4

The giving of the Holy Spirit on the same moedim as the giving of the Torah is the standard of new life, absolutely unequaled anywhere. Consider these words of promise from Ezekiel:

> I will give you a new heart and put a new spirit within you; and I will remove the heart of stone from your flesh and give you a heart of flesh. I will put My Spirit within you and cause you to walk in My statutes, and you will be careful to observe My ordinances.
>
> —EZEKIEL 36:26–27

Can there be any doubt that Torah and Holy Spirit belong together? Can a man in his natural state follow the Torah appropriately? Apparently not! However, the redeemed, guided by the Holy Spirit, can walk in newness of life, just as Paul taught:

> What shall we say then? Are we to continue in sin so that grace may increase? May it never be! How shall we who died to sin still live in it? Or do you not know that all of us who have been baptized into Christ Jesus have been baptized into His death? Therefore we have been buried with Him through baptism into death, so that as Christ was raised from the dead through the glory of the Father, so we too might walk in newness of life. For if we have become united with Him in the likeness of His death, certainly we shall also be in the likeness of His resurrection, knowing this, that our old self was crucified with Him, in order that our body of sin might be done away with, so that we would no longer be slaves to sin; for he who has died is freed from sin.
>
> —ROMANS 6:1–7

This is also clear in the new covenant Jeremiah defined for us:

> "Behold, days are coming," declares the LORD, "when I will make a new covenant with the house of Israel and with the house of Judah, not like the covenant which I made with their fathers in the day I took them by the hand to bring them out of the land of Egypt, My covenant which they broke, although I was a husband to them," declares the LORD. "But this is the covenant which I will make with the house of Israel after those days," declares the LORD, "I will put My law within them and on their heart I will write it; and I will be

their God, and they shall be My people. They will not teach again, each man his neighbor and each man his brother, saying, 'Know the LORD,' for they will all know Me, from the least of them to the greatest of them," declares the LORD, "for I will forgive their iniquity, and their sin I will remember no more."

—JEREMIAH 31:31–34

Notice that in the new covenant God says, "I will put My law within them and on their heart I will write it." This is the principal work of the Holy Spirit in our lives: to write the Torah on our hearts. This is the purpose of the fourth moedim in month three. This is the standard that brings forth new life! As a chiastic model of the seven days of Creation and the seven appointed times suggests, this is the central point of the whole biblical message for wholeness of life. Our God intends to write the divinely designed and divinely revealed instructions of the Torah on our hearts by the power of the Holy Spirit, making us a free people.

Once this standard of new life is set, we are ready to conquer months four, five, and six, gathering much and joyously looking forward to month seven as a time to rest and rejoice in and with our Creator and fellow man.

I close with this confidence: if you will purposefully apply the biblical calendar to your life, you will see amazing things. You will fulfill your purpose as a created being, created in the image of God!

NOTES

CHAPTER 4:
NATURAL RHYTHMS VS. REVELATION KNOWLEDGE

1. Strong's Concordance, s.v. "moedim," H4150.

CHAPTER 7:
FINDING THE END OF THE SEVENTH YEAR

1. William Greider, *Secrets of the Temple: How the Federal Reserve Runs the Country* (New York: Simon & Schuster, 1989).

CHAPTER 9:
THE TRANSITION FROM SEVEN TO ONE

1. Strong's Concordance, s.v. "echad," H259.
2. Ibid., s.v. "ri'shown," H7223.

CHAPTER 13:
THE LIVING CREATURES, SURPRISE AND DANGER

1. Strong's Concordance, s.v. "nephesh chay," H5315 and H2416.

SELECTED BIBLIOGRAPHY

Alewine, Hollisa. The Creation Gospel, website, www. thecreationgospel.com.

Benner, Jeff A. Ancient Hebrew Research Center, website, www.ancient-hebrew.org.

Cahill, Thomas. *Desire of the Everlasting Hills.* New York: Nan A. Talese/Doubleday, 2001.

———. *The Gifts of the Jews: How a Tribe of Desert Nomads Changed the Way Everyone Thinks and Feels.* New York: Nan A. Talese/Doubleday, 1998.

———. *How the Irish Saved Civilization: The Untold Story of Ireland's Heroic Role From the Fall of Rome to the Rise of Medieval Europe.* New York: Nan A. Talese/ Doubleday, 1995.

Kass, Leon R. *The Beginning of Wisdom.* Chicago: University of Chicago Press, 2006.

Moody, Valerie. *The Feasts of Adonai, Why Christians Should Look at the Biblical Feasts.* Lubbock, TX: Gibbora Productions, 2009.

ABOUT the AUTHOR

BARRY MILLER IS fifty-five years old and has been married for thirty years to the love of his life, Audrey. They have two college-aged children.

As a businessman, he has been actively involved in owning and managing MVE Group Inc., an electronic security and electrical contracting firm, for about thirty years. He served as its CEO from 2010 to 2014.

Additionally, Barry has volunteered on a number of local boards and foundations within the local community and region.

He is an Adult Bible Fellowship teacher at Lancaster Evangelical Free Church in Lititz, Pennsylvania, where he also serves as an elder, usher, and a liaison to a local Messianic Jewish congregation.

CONTACT the AUTHOR

E-mail: barry@7and5orhymes.com

Website: 7and5orhymes.com